the Denver
FOLK MUSIC
TRADITION

the Denver
FOLK MUSIC
TRADITION
An Unplugged History,
from Harry Tuft to Swallow Hill and Beyond

Paul Malkoski
FOREWORDS *by* HARRY TUFT & TOM SCHARF

Charleston   London

THE
History
PRESS

Published by The History Press
Charleston, SC 29403
www.historypress.net

Copyright © 2012 by Paul Malkoski
All rights reserved

Cover image: Swallow Hill Marques. *Nick Annis.*

First published 2012

Manufactured in the United States

ISBN 978.1.60949.532.9

Library of Congress Cataloging-in-Publication Data

Malkoski, Paul A.
The Denver folk music tradition : an unplugged history, from Harry Tuft to Swallow Hill
and beyond / Paul Malkoski.
p. cm.
ISBN 978-1-60949-532-9
1. Folk music--Colorado--Denver--History and criticism. I. Title.
ML3551.8.D46M36 2012
2012001588

CONTENTS

Forewords, by Harry Tuft and Tom Scharf   7
Preface   11

1. Beginnings   15
2. Music in the Mountains   21
3. The Denver Folklore Center   31
4. Swallow Hill Music Association: Stayin' Alive   57
5. Swallow Hill—A New Home   69
6. A Changing of the Guard   83
7. A Change Is Gonna Come   105
8. The Future's So Bright   113
9. Bringing It All Back Home: The Community   133

Bibliography   143
Index   149
About the Author   159

FOREWORDS

C ommunity. That's what it's all about.

I didn't know it when I first got interested in folk music (the dreaded "F" word). I had just returned to my classes at Dartmouth College after a summer of travel, during which time I began learning guitar and understanding its two additional bass strings, which differentiate it from my baritone uke. I heard that there was a folk song club on campus, and upon joining, I learned that it had booked Pete Seeger for a concert. He arrived in town in the afternoon for a meeting of the club, before his evening concert. His message to us was simple: go out into the surrounding area and seek out folks who make music, "collect" them and perhaps start a festival with them. I believe that his underlying message was that music is a medium that brings folks together, that community is so important to our survival and we need music in our lives.

Music pleases, music binds, music heals, music brings joy and eases sorrow. What greater reward than to be a vehicle through which music is spread? I'm forever grateful for that.

Harry Tuft
November 2011

"Hear" for a moment

We are always in a unique moment in time. Throughout our lives, significant events and experiences creep in to subtly remind us of this fact. Sometimes they hit us like a freight train. Music is such an experience. I see it every day.

Some may say that music is not the soundtrack to their lives, just the background notes between here and there. But who has not been moved by taps playing at a funeral? Who has not had a reaction to "The Star-Spangled Banner" at a ballgame? Who has not remembered a spiritual song like "Amazing Grace" or seized an anthem to represent their transition into young adulthood?

People have always found places to gather to share common, transformative experiences. Music has been central, if not the exclusive focus, to a majority of these gatherings, from the fires on the plains of the Serengeti, to the arenas of Ancient Greece, to town squares, churches, coffee shops and Central Park.

The *place* is central to the experience, but there has to be an *environment*, or *culture*, in that place to help channel the experience—not manage or control it but help facilitate and encourage it, to make sure that everyone feels equal, part of the transformation. Daily, I witness the special dynamic when music is shared person to person, among a group or within our community. It becomes amplified somehow, and we want more.

People like Harry Tuft at the Denver Folklore Center and the folks at Swallow Hill Music understand this power and help to facilitate it. There is recognition that the collective musical experience is much bigger than the sum of its parts. The simultaneous human transformation that happens during a musical performance or while learning to play an instrument brings an honest, true joy to people—and it somehow cements us together.

The feeling is profound, often euphoric, sometimes sad and always human. Being in touch with this "humanness" is humbling. And there is a quiet reverence you give to this time, when you have passed through this moment aware—and changed.

This book is about the power of music and community in Colorado. But it happens all over the globe, and it's comforting to know that we are connected in a bigger, important way. From my seat in Denver, I am thankful that there are people like Harry Tuft who help make this happen. And I'm thankful that I am one of the stewards of the mission that embodies Swallow Hill Music.

We are just a few in a long line of people who are here for a moment to share or teach a song. We know that the music lasts longer than we do—and we are glad for it.

I believe that in this busy, crazy world, people crave this interaction more than ever. In an era when music is too often a *thing*—more commoditized than ever, sold in bits and bytes—we still keep gathering in *places* to share it on the most elemental level. These are the places I like to be.

Tom Scharf
December 2011

PREFACE

As a boy growing up in western Kentucky, I knew at some level I was different from the other kids. Like most youngsters in the 1950s, I chose up sides for sandlot baseball games, played cowboys and Indians in the nearby woods, watched Walt Disney's Davy Crockett movies at our neighborhood theater and viewed Saturday morning cartoons and shoot-'em-ups on television. Music was always special to me, though my family was not particularly musical. My mother played a little piano as a girl, and my father played trumpet (by ear, no less!) in his high school band, but there were no instruments in our house and precious little money for lessons of any kind. My mother regularly listened to the radio as she went about her housework, and when I was nearby, I paid close attention to the pop tunes that poured out—pop, country and early rock-and-roll. It was all there in those days before Clear Channel took over and radio became obsessed with market segmentation and cost control. On our all-too-infrequent car trips (my father worked six days a week as assistant manager of a department store), I often stood on the transmission hump in the back seat (seat belts were years away) with my attention riveted on the sounds floating out of the glowing dashboard radio. I was too young to be discerning; I listened to and liked it all.

Sometime in the late 1950s, my father brought home a record player, an early portable RCA stereo that looked like a beige suitcase. It rested on a metal frame in our living room, the turntable folded down in the middle exposing the controls, while the speakers swung out from the sides like a set of ears, and it played these newfangled $33^{1}/3$ rpm long-play albums in stereo! Unlike my playmates—though I didn't realize it at the time—I sat in front of the magic box and listened to whatever albums my father had purchased, mostly big bands like Guy Lombardo, vocal groups like the Ink Spots and Broadway musicals or movie scores. I had my favorite albums, including the soundtrack from *Around the World in Eighty Days*, which I would play over and over and over again, much to my mother's chagrin. She liked the music but didn't care much for the tedious repetition.

I memorized the lyrics to popular songs and sang them to myself as I walked the mile to school or rode my bike to see my school chums. I have vivid memories of lying in my bed by the window on the second floor of our little house on hot, muggy summer evenings, watching and listening to thunderstorms boil up and sweep in, dumping cooling rain on the mighty oak trees outside. And singing songs to myself, thinking no one could hear. One summer morning, a neighbor asked if it had been me singing "Sixteen Tons" the evening before and then complimented my singing after my mother responded that it was. I wasn't sure what to make of it.

We didn't have much in the way of disposable cash, but my father was committed to seeing his kids get a Catholic education. Like my schoolmates, I sang in the choir and at Mass but usually found the music boring. Our small school had a limited music program taught entirely by Sister Mary Agnes. About that time, I wanted to learn guitar, but Sister Mary Agnes knew nothing about the instrument, so it remained beyond my reach. Private lessons and an instrument were not within my family's budgetary reach.

Outside of school, I was caught up in the birth throes of rock-and-roll, and who could blame me? We lived 170 miles north of Memphis, and Elvis Presley had hit locally like a windstorm with "That's All Right Mama" long before the rest of the nation took notice. I have a vivid memory of a local deejay playing "Hound Dog" over and over again for half an hour one day. I was in heaven. My mother was bewildered. The family gathered in the living room when Elvis made his first national television appearance on Milton Berle's *Texaco Star Theater*, where he bounced and gyrated across the stage, scandalizing parents everywhere.

When I first heard "Tom Dooley" on the radio, I was entranced. It must have been the simple sound of banjos and guitars that pulled at me, begging me to pay attention. As folk music's popularity grew, I found myself more interested in it than in rock-and-roll, but not to the exclusion of rock. There was (still is) something genuine in the simplicity, in the stories so many folk songs tell and in the beauty of unadorned acoustic instruments. It was 1963 when the folk music bug finally enveloped me. After seeing Ian and Sylvia and Judy Collins for the first time on television, I knew I had to see if I could do what they were doing—singing and playing guitar. I purchased albums by both and again sat transfixed in front of the stereo, playing them continuously, absorbing as much as my musically untrained but eager mind could take in. Weeks later, at the age of seventeen, I bought a cheap Lindell guitar, a Mel Bay guitar instruction book and a Kingston Trio songbook and set out to see if I could ever learn to make music.

A few years later, I found myself living in New York but still without any friends who knew anything about music. I was somewhat shy and a little intimidated by the big city and had not put myself into situations where I might meet other players. At best, I was a poor guitarist and an unpolished singer, but I loved trying to figure out the guitar's mysteries and spent nearly all my disposable cash on records. I read everything I could get my hands on, including the bible of folk music, *Sing Out! The Folk Music Magazine*, devouring every word of every issue, including the ads. Through sheer good fortune (karma?), I fell in with a couple of musicians who were gracious and patient enough to let me sit in with them and their friends at informal picking sessions. After nearly every song, I pestered them with questions: "How did you do that lick?" and "Where did you learn that song?" They tolerated my ragged playing and often stopped mid-song to point out that I had lost the beat, showing me how to find it and how to hold it. It was embarrassing at times, but it was more helpful than anything else I had experienced musically.

By now, if you've read this far you might be thinking, "Where's he going with this? What does this have to do with folk music history? Or Denver?" My own musical odyssey simply illustrates one person's musical trek and is likely not typical. But it illustrates something that I found missing from the 1960s New York folk music scene: support and safe haven. Profit and stardom drove much of the city's music scene then as it does now. Many notable musicians came to New York to seek their fortunes, including Judy Collins, Bob Dylan, Phil Ochs and a host of others whose names are lost to most of us now. If you had real talent, if you could fit in with the big boys and girls, you were part of New York's folk community. If you were not of that caliber, there were few places to find musical camaraderie and explore music for personal pleasure.

Denver is different and largely unique in providing support and safe haven for acoustic music lovers. Swallow Hill Music Association grew out of such a need. The hardy, and sometimes naïve, founders of Swallow Hill created an organization they hoped would carry on the nurturing environment all had experienced at Harry Tuft's Denver Folklore Center (DFC). Personal profit was not the motivator for Swallow Hill's founders; it was the need to preserve the music community that had first coalesced around the DFC, the place where many of them had taken lessons; bought books, strings and instruments; and heard the best professional performers in the field. Most of all, it was where they felt like part of a family that shared an overarching passion for this thing called folk music. Ego was not important; the music was.

And it still is. There are a few similar organizations around the country that present similar musical fare: Chicago's Old Town School of Folk Music, Ann Arbor's the Ark and Boston's Club Passim. These establishments keep musical traditions alive with solid, creative musical education facilities. Having survived the boom and bust of the folk revival, these institutions keep the spirit going by providing a community atmosphere in which all aspects of music are accessible.

This book grew from a fortuitous Colorado history assignment in graduate school but turned into a labor of love fueled by passion for music and community. Unlike many more formal and academic histories in which the narrative thread relies on extensive research in library stacks around the country, I drew much of my research from the memories of those who established, fed, managed and contributed to Swallow Hill. The story isn't mine; it belongs to the Swallow Hill community—those musicians, audiences, teachers, students and volunteers bound together by a common passion.

I am indebted to many people who helped me during the gestation of this book. Dr. Tom Noel was the first to encourage me to write about Harry Tuft and the Denver Folklore Center, and Harry was gracious enough to sit patiently for hours of interviews and endless questions. Dozens of Swallow Hill members, executive directors, teachers and volunteers told me their stories, all with passion and insight. They appear in the text. Tom Scharf gave me encouragement and support when it looked like things would never get off the ground, and Meg Ivey searched through the photos in Swallow Hill's archives. My wife, Mim, encouraged the nascent writer in me, recognizing the ability long before I believed in it. This history would not exist were it not for all the members of the Swallow Hill community who, through more than three decades, have kept the music and family alive.

I hope you will forgive gaps in the story and lapses in accuracy. Any errors are mine.

1

Beginnings

On a sunny day in the late 1960s, a scraggly, rumpled-looking Vietnam veteran walked into the Denver Folklore Center at East Seventeenth Avenue and Pearl Street. It was a typical bustling business day for the DFC: young people coming and going to their guitar lessons; others, usually older, simply hanging out, passionately arguing the virtues of new versus vintage Martin guitars; and still others buying strings and picks or thumbing through bins of folk records. Harry Tuft, the Folklore Center's owner and proprietor, barely noticed the vet, recognizing the man as an occasional visitor who did not usually engage in the regular flow of conversation, a man who seemed a bit strange.

By this time, the Folklore Center had become the mecca for Denver's acoustic musicians, a place unlike contemporary music stores. Tuft opened his doors in 1962, at a time when music stores usually meant pianos and band instruments. If they sold guitars or stringed instruments at all, it was not much more than an annoying sideline for the commissioned salespeople. Customers came to the Folklore Center as much to talk as to buy; the atmosphere centered more on camaraderie than commerce. People came to share their excitement about nonconformist music and felt as if they were part of something special, like being in on a hip joke the mainstream had not quite gotten. Tuft, never one to oversell, encouraged customers to try out instruments and find the ones that suited their requirements rather than the ones he needed to sell. Customers—in twos and threes—might fall into an impromptu jam if the tune and the time seemed appropriate. If one word could describe the DFC, it was "comfortable."

Tuft and some of the DFC regulars knew the veteran, who would come in but not take part in the goings-on. He seemed perhaps a bit more agitated than usual, but the young men coming home from that faraway war often appeared tormented by ghosts others could not fathom. The regulars that day hardly noticed him as the conversation ebbed and flowed. Until he pulled a pistol from his coat pocket.

Pistols were never a common sight at the DFC. The mild-mannered Tuft was as surprised as anyone, at first thinking it might just be a sick joke and then realizing that the situation was far more serious. Not knowing any better, perhaps just innocent enough to know he had to do something—anything—he began to talk to the veteran, who slowly responded to Tuft's calm voice. Who knows how long it took? Two minutes? Five minutes? Thirty seconds? Tuft recalled, "He ended up weeping…that's what happened then. I forget if he gave me the gun or just put it away and walked out. I'm sure that these kids, whoever they are—as old as they are now—still remember that. But it was that kind of place."

It was *that* kind of place. Not that gun-waving Vietnam vets came in every day, but people of all kinds, of all ages, from all walks of life found refuge in the funky, and normally calm, confines of the Denver Folklore Center. They might buy a little something—a set of strings, some picks, a record or a book—but buying was often an afterthought, perhaps something people felt compelled to do. But neither Tuft nor his customers seemed to place an emphasis on commerce; it was more about community in a time of turmoil.

I AM A LONESOME RAMBLER

Harry Tuft had not set out to be a merchant, much less a community builder. He was born in 1935, raised in Philadelphia, Pennsylvania, and attended West Philadelphia High School. His Jewish father, a doctor, and his mother, a social worker, had hoped their son might go into medicine. After graduating with a degree in philosophy from Dartmouth College and two years of postgraduate work in architecture at the University of Pennsylvania, it was clear he had other dreams in mind. Like others in the mid- and late 1950s, Tuft had become infatuated with folk music. He had taken piano and clarinet lessons as a child and began plunking the ukulele when he was thirteen. Before long, he traded his four-string baritone uke for a six-string guitar and began performing for youth groups and hanging around the Gilded Cage, Philly's popular folk music coffeehouse. Through his participation in the Sunday hoots at the Gilded Cage, Tuft became friends with Dick Weissman, a talented banjo and guitar player, who soon moved to New York City to find paying work as a studio musician. Weissman would play a critical role in Tuft's "folk education."

Tuft, like many of his college contemporaries, acquired his introduction to folk music from the Weavers. The popular quartet—Pete Seeger, Lee Hays, Fred Hellerman and Ronnie Gilbert—had rocketed to fame in 1951, when they charted "Kisses Sweeter than Wine" and "Goodnight Irene." But it did not last. The 1950s were strange and contradictory times for folk music in New York and America. Folk music had first gained popularity with urban audiences through efforts of the New Left to connect with the working class. No artist personified the working-class connection better than Woody Guthrie. Born to an Oklahoma socialist father, the young singer Guthrie became radicalized through his connections with the California branch of the Communist Party of the United States of America (CPUSA) in the late 1930s. In 1940, he moved to New York City, where he became the darling of the Left and the poet of the downtrodden. Guthrie fell in with a group of performers who shared a belief that America could be a better place for the common man. His singing partners often included Pete Seeger, Cisco Houston and Bess Lomax; he counted actors Burl Ives and Will Geer as fans and friends.

Guthrie served in the Merchant Marines during World War II, when he had two ships torpedoed under him, but by the mid-1950s, he was too ill to perform regularly. McCarthyism and Cold War fears had driven other radical singers, including Pete Seeger and the members of the Weavers, underground and off the airwaves, but not before they had touched millions, especially high school and college students, with their lusty singing and playing. Harry Tuft was among those students inspired by the Weavers to take up folk music. Nonetheless, popular music, in spite of the emergence of rock-and-roll, was hardly revolutionary.

No one is quite sure why a mostly urban America embraced rural folk music. Sociologists, historians and journalists have speculated that it was a form of cultural rebellion, a reaction to the pedestrian pop music dominating the charts during the Eisenhower era. Others have postulated that it was the beginning of the splintering of mass culture. Still others feel that it reflected a need to connect to something perceived as more authentic, more *real*. None of these explanations is entirely satisfactory or free of speculation. Historians often rely on the comments of participants for whom the music meant the most. For them, there was something in music based on ancient and rural roots that spoke more to the human condition than the Tin Pan Alley hits, which appeared to be manufactured, tailored to meet public acceptance. Arguments aside, folk music was, like the Beats, an underground phenomenon, not typically found in the mainstream.

There was something decidedly bohemian about folk music, and no place was more attuned to it than New York's Greenwich Village, home in the late 1950s to a budding folk community. Jazz, with its jangly energy, intellectual stance and atonal rebellion, was the public musical face of the Beat Generation, but folk music was the Beats' communal meeting ground. Performers vied for attention in smoky clubs and recorded when they could for small record labels dedicated to noncommercial musical styles. All that changed in 1958, when the Kingston Trio scored a number one smash hit with "Tom Dooley." Folk music reemerged—defanged of its left leanings and scrubbed clean—as a form of mainstream entertainment.

In 1960, Tuft made his first trip to New York City to visit his friend Dick Weissman and to sample firsthand the folk culture of Greenwich Village. Weissman took him to visit Izzy Young's New York Folklore Center, whose key concepts Harry would carry to the West.

Few characters in what is now called the folk revival were more seminally important and harder to label than Izzy Young. He was not a performer, artist manager or record company executive, and his Folklore Center was unique. Opened in 1957 at 110 MacDougal Street, just a short walk from Washington Square, the center became important to the folk revival. "Locally and nationally, the Folklore Center became a locus for folk music, supplying books, records, new and used instruments and all sorts of information, and offering performers and fans a convenient gathering place," historian Ronald D. Cohen noted. In his cramped, musty store, Young occasionally presented performances by new and emerging, as well as established, folk artists, while peddling his eclectic collection of instruments, records and books.

Later in 1960, Tuft and Weissman made a trip to Chicago, where Weissman was scheduled to meet with the director of the Old Town School of Folk Music. There, Harry saw another aspect of the folk revival not present in the Village. Founded in 1957, the Old Town School of Folk Music was—and remains today—the largest school of its kind, offering lessons to eager students wanting to learn guitar, banjo, mandolin, songwriting, folk dance and nearly anything associated with folk music and visiting musicians offering workshops on a variety of topics and skills, as well as providing live performances four or five nights a week. At this center of Chicago's budding folk community, Tuft saw his future.

In December of that same year, Tuft traveled west to Colorado with Weissman, who was on his way to Los Angles to perform. Harry landed a job in Georgetown at the Holy Cat, a small ski lodge. He was able to pursue his passion for skiing at A-Basin during the day and spent most of his evenings at the Holy Cat bussing tables, sweeping the floor and toiling in the kitchen in the hopes of having a few minutes to perform for guests at the end of the night. In 1961, he and his girlfriend found work at the Berthoud Pass Lodge, enjoying the chance to ski the Rockies but making little money. After the ski season ended, they worked for a while in Aspen as housekeepers and then traveled to the West Coast, where Tuft drove a cab for the Sausalito Taxi Company and looked for opportunities to perform. By chance, he met up again with Dick Weissman, who by this time was playing with John Phillips (later of the Mamas and the Papas fame) in a popular folk group, the Journeymen, which was playing at San Francisco's Hungry i.

Tuft performed at the Hungry i as well, singing and playing his guitar. Paying music jobs were few, and Tuft came to the realization that performance, while satisfying, was not likely to be his full-time career. He had auditioned for Hal Neustaedter, owner of the Denver folk club the Exodus. Since its opening in 1959, all manner of performers had appeared there, including Judy Collins, the Smothers Brothers and the Kingston Trio. Neustaedter had a good eye for talent, and the word was that if he liked you, you had a good chance to succeed. Unfortunately, he was not bowled over by Harry's performance. Tuft began to consider the possibility of a store that would combine the commercial merchandising of the New York Folklore Center with the teaching and performance setting of Chicago's Old Town School of Folk Music. Neustaedter encouraged Harry to consider Denver for his enterprise. Tuft returned to the East Coast and began making plans. Naïve about business, Tuft used his meager life savings of $900 to purchase stock from Izzy Young (mostly obscure things Izzy knew he would never sell), packed his belongings into a 1951 Dodge panel truck and set out on the return trip west. He arrived in Denver in December 1961.

2

MUSIC IN THE MOUNTAINS

S ince Denver's founding in 1859 in the foothills of the Rocky Mountains, music of all forms contributed significantly to shaping its cultural landscape. Music proved popular in early Denver saloons. From its earliest days, Denver citizens seeking "real" culture in a tough mining town were able to enjoy opera and classical music at such landmark sites as the Tabor Grand Opera House. Never a jazz hotbed on a par with Kansas City or New Orleans, Denver's Five Points nevertheless boasted clubs where both local and national artists performed. In the 1950s and '60s, like many urban centers across America, Denver experienced an explosion in the popularity of folk music as such artists as the Kingston Trio and Peter, Paul and Mary charted a string of radio hits. Interested listeners caught folk music in a wide variety of venues, from the simplest clubs and bars to major concert halls, and that array represented a measurement of how the public accepted—and supported—the genre. In most respects, Denver's folk scene mirrored that of other American cities, yet it proved unique in many ways.

WHERE IT ALL BEGAN

Folk music emerged as a commercial phenomenon for the first time in urban America in the 1950s. Before the Eisenhower years, folk music was little more than a curio, an oddity that held little interest for America's dominantly urban population, who generally preferred the Tin Pan Alley pop music found in their bars, on the radio and on television. What many now understand as folk music (at least in a narrow, Anglo-Saxon orientation)—that is, music based on the Scottish-Irish-English song forms generally associated with the people of the Appalachian American Southeast—held little appeal to the sophisticated ears of urban America in the 1930s and '40s.

Ralph Peer produced the first commercially successful sound recordings of folk and country music in 1927 in Bristol, Tennessee. Peer had a knack for "discovering" rural musicians, and on one of his many trips to the Southland he recorded the Carter Family (A.P., wife Sarah and Maybelle) and Jimmie Rodgers, "the Singing Brakeman." While they all hoped to make money, Peer intended to sell his records to rural listeners, for he believed their appeal was strictly limited to those regions. Similarly, other recording companies released 78rpm disks of black country-blues artists for sale to African Americans. These recordings, known in the trade as "race records," seldom found listeners outside black neighborhoods until after World War II.

The Communist Party of the United States of America (CPUSA) and the New Left played a surprisingly central role in bringing rural music to urban centers. One of the most noted and widely respected scholars of protest music, R. Serge Denisoff, wrote extensively of the history of folk music and its association with the American Left. Before the wide commercialization of folk music began in the 1950s and '60s, the urban public perceived folk music as much a foreign culture as songs in other languages. Denisoff went on to say, "The Folk Consciousness of the 'Old Left' refers to an awareness of folk music which leads to its use in a foreign (urban) environment in the framework of social, economic, or political action." The awareness of folk music as a viable medium came slowly to the Old Left. The CPUSA idealization of folk song nearly paralleled that of the Nazis in Germany. The adoption of folk songs was, in many ways, curious since "social crusaders historically have relied upon songs that were familiar to their potential audiences," writes Denisoff, and most urban audiences had no particular desire to identify with rural musical forms.

Foreign-born members dominated the CPUSA, at least until the late 1930s; only one-seventh of the twenty thousand American Communists spoke English. As such, they and other left wing movements tended to favor the songs they had learned in the home, the church or especially the "old country," few of which were likely to attract new adherents. Isolation from the masses greatly hindered the growth of the CPUSA, something that appears to have been a major source of irritation in Moscow. Connection to the masses—and folk music—came through two significant sources: strikes in the southern coal fields and textile mills and a young singer/songwriter, Woody Guthrie.

The 1929 strikes at the Loray textile mill in Gastonia, North Carolina, brought the urban-centered CPUSA into contact with a grass-roots union movement. The CPUSA interpreted the confrontation between striking workers and the company town of Gastonia as a textbook example of the Marxist image of ruthless capitalists exploiting a tormented proletariat. The CPUSA heard, perhaps for the first time, American folk song forms used to exhort the strikers. At about the same time, coal men, striking in Bell and Harlan Counties in eastern Kentucky, provided more vivid examples of radical song, even more surprising for the CPUSA because the most literate and powerful of the singers was a woman, not a miner. Mrs. Florence Reece, wife of a coal miner, was the initial source of radical song. Following a number of attacks by "gun thugs" and the local sheriff, Reece, so the story goes, ripped a sheet from a wall calendar and wrote a song about the combatants of bloody Harlan County:

They say in Harlan County,
There are no neutrals there:
You'll either be a union man
Or a thug for J.H. Blair.

Don't scab for the bosses,
Don't listen to their lies.
Us poor folks haven't got a chance
Unless we organize.
Which side are you on?

It was not long before Reece and others traveled to New York to assist in union organization, their songs and voices seen as tools to encourage the downtrodden. In time, a small but talented community of singing country people found homes amidst the radical New York Left.

Three thousand miles away on the West Coast, Woody Guthrie had acquired a radio audience among the Okies and other rural people displaced by the Great Depression and the Dust Bowl. Guthrie, the rough-edged but talented son of an Oklahoma socialist, had landed a job on the Los Angeles radio station KFVD and connected to the many newcomers from the depressed South. In 1939, Guthrie wrote a song about onetime labor leader Tom Mooney, who had just won his release after twenty-two years in prison.

That song brought Guthrie to the attention of the local CPUSA chapter, which employed him at rallies and meetings. His exposure to the CPUSA and his travels in 1939–40 to the work and migrant camps sharpened Guthrie's populist feelings, which he began to express forcefully in song. But while his songs were by and of the workingman, Guthrie was anything but a doctrinal dogmatist; he was simply too restless and undisciplined—and too ornery—to become a religionist for the Left.

Guthrie hitchhiked to New York City in 1940 at the request of Will Geer, the actor and activist and leading spokesman of the "folk" agitprop school. Geer, a graduate of the University of Chicago who had attended Columbia and Oxford as a graduate student, was acting in a Broadway play. Geer's primary historical contribution to the proletarian renaissance was his ability to recruit "raggedy-assed" singers into the so-called radical scene of New York City. He helped to organize fundraisers for a variety of leftist causes and introduced the young Burl Ives to New York City, where he performed for various affairs. Guthrie fell in with Geer and activist singer Pete Seeger, working in such groups as the loosely knit Almanac Singers before World War II took Seeger to the army and Guthrie to the Merchant Marines.

Historian R. Serge Denisoff noted that the folk song renaissance was "collectively oriented" and that the performers of the time were perceived as part of the collective. "The collective ethos of the period minimized the importance of the individual performer." For example, no member of the Almanac Singers, including Guthrie and Seeger, was given public credit for his songwriting abilities. Singers like Guthrie, Seeger and Negro blues artists Josh White and Huddie "Lead Belly" Ledbetter performed at rent parties (designed to collect a bit of cash to pay rent), rallies and other functions as much to make a dollar as to establish a political view.

Folk music remained limited in its appeal into the 1940s, largely due to World War II, when most of the New Left buried their more revolutionary ideals and sang patriotic songs supporting U.S. war efforts. When Hitler attacked Russia, many on the Left joined the service. When the war ended, folk musicians sought to find new ways to express themselves—and make a living—but the public failed to embrace their initial offerings. Seeger and Guthrie published *The People's Song Book* in 1948 and joined other left-wing artists in supporting Henry Wallace's unsuccessful run at the presidency, but this did little to advance their careers.

In 1949, banjoist Pete Seeger teamed up with Lee Hays (bass vocals), Fred Hellerman (guitar) and Ronnie Gilbert (vocals) to form the Weavers, their name intended to honor the hardworking textile laborers. They worked

Though blacklisted from television after the Red Scare in the 1950s, Pete Seeger maintained a busy worldwide performance schedule. Harry Tuft presented him a number of times. The Denver Folklore Center.

hard to create a clean-cut image and presented a wide array of folk songs of America and other countries. They found amazing local success during a six-month engagement at the Village Gate in 1950, which led to Decca Records signing them to a recording contract in 1951. Their first single release, the joyful Hebrew folk song "Tzena Tzena" (backed with Lead Belly's "Good Night Irene"), shot up the charts and sold more than 250,000 copies. Arguably, the popular folk revival started here. Other acts, like the Tarriers and the Gateway Singers, tried to follow, but the Red Scare, brought on through the HUAC hearings and Senator Joseph McCarthy, put a quick end to it all. By 1952, the commie-baiting magazine *Red Channels* had accused the members of the Weavers of Communist ties, even though their music was markedly apolitical. It didn't matter. Seeger appeared before HUAC, where he refused to answer questions based on his First Amendment rights of free speech. By 1953, the Weavers were blacklisted out of business.

But the Weavers' music proved broadly influential. Young college students, especially on the East and West Coasts, including a young Harry Tuft, listened to the Weavers and took up guitars and banjos, making music of their own based on American and ethnic songs. While the Red Scare put the Weavers on the sidelines, it did not stop the folk revival; it simply drove it to a commercial underground. In 1958, the Kingston Trio—Bob Shane, Dave Guard and Nick Reynolds—topped the charts with the most unlikely hit, "Tom Dooley," and the popular folk revival suddenly bloomed full force. By 1962, borrowing liberally from such sources as Pete Seeger, Woody Guthrie and the Weavers, dozens of popular folk artists (including the Brothers Four, the Limelighters, the Journeymen, the Highwaymen and Peter, Paul and Mary) followed the Kingston Trio up the charts, proving folk music to be a popular alternative to mainstream offerings.

EAST, WEST AND IN BETWEEN

If the folk revival could claim a nerve center, New York City's Greenwich Village leads all other candidates. Long the home of the bohemian set, the Village boasted numerous nightclubs, including the Bitter End, the Village Gate (known as much for jazz as for folk), Gerde's Folk City and the Gaslight, all of which featured folk artists in the mid- to late 1950s. Unlike any other place, New York City was the home of record labels (Folkways, Elektra, Vanguard, Riverside and Stinson) primarily dedicated to recording and releasing folk music on a regular basis. Likewise, the Village possessed a somewhat unique business in Izzy Young's New York Folklore Center, which, in addition to selling musical instruments, books and sheet music, acted as a clearinghouse for all things related to folk music. Young often presented live performances in his own cramped facilities, as well as at other venues in New York City.

On the tier just below New York City, folk music thrived in Boston, where activities centered on Cambridge at Club 47, and on the West Coast, folk music flourished in the clubs of Los Angeles (the Ash Grove and the Troubadour) and San Francisco (the Hungry i and the Purple Onion). In Chicago, the Old Town School of Folk Music placed an emphasis on teaching music skills while bringing dozens of prominent performers (Josh White, Pete Seeger and Big Bill Broonzy) to the Windy City.

DENVER'S EARLY FOLK SCENE

While not as vibrant as New York, Boston or the West Coast, Denver's nascent folk scene resembled that of other major city centers. As folk music gained in popularity, club owners willingly booked the occasional folk music act, as long as the artist possessed a certain commercial appeal and some national recognition. Folk music was, after all, a segment of the music business, with the emphasis on business. In 1959, local impresario Hal Neustaedter founded the Exodus, Denver's most notable folk club, at 1999 Lincoln Street, where patrons descended a short flight of stairs into a dimly lit area of crowded tables and chairs that held perhaps one hundred listeners. One longtime Denver resident, when recalling the Exodus, remembered that the club proved popular, in part, because eighteen-year-olds could get in for two dollars and buy cheap pitchers of beer while seeing acts like the Smothers Brothers on their first national tour. Like other clubs around the country, the Exodus featured national acts but also gave opportunities to promising locals.

HOT TIMES AT THE CLUBS

While the most popular and visible acts played the biggest and most famous rooms, the Denver club scene enjoyed its own renaissance. Though the Exodus faded into memory, other club owners stepped in over time and offered

The Satire Lounge on East Colfax, known for its margaritas, was home to live music during the late 1950s and early '60s when Walt Conley hosted numerous folk music performances. *Tom Noel.*

an array of environments and musical palettes. In the 1960s, Walt Conley played a pivotal role. An African American singer noted for his repertoire of Irish ballads, an actor and a storyteller, Conley secured performers for the Satire Lounge, a Mexican restaurant run by Greek restaurateur Pete Contos on East Colfax Avenue, where he often performed. Conley, a seriously funny man, frequently allowed performers to walk in off the street and audition to be the evening's opening act. Conley left Denver to pursue an acting career in Los Angeles but returned in the 1980s and opened a club called Conley's Nostalgia on South Broadway, where he continued to host folk music, often in conjunction with Swallow Hill Music Association, until he retired in 1994. Conley passed away in 2003.

The old Green Spider gained its reputation as one of Denver's beatnik hangouts, its décor dominated by fat waxy candles on the tables and very little other light. Brightly woven Mexican gods' eyes decorated the scene. People sat around and jammed. The Green Spider closed its doors in 1967.

Other significant Denver clubs included Ebbets Field and the Regency Room. In the 1970s, Ebbets Field, named after the Brooklyn Dodgers' old home stadium, operated in the Executive Tower Inn, then one of the trendier new high-rises in the early stages of downtown Denver's revitalization. Patrons walked down a few stairs into a rectangular space containing mini tables and about 150 seats in a generally noisy environment. In many ways, Ebbets replaced the Exodus as the main popular music-oriented nightclub in Denver, booking an eclectic array of acts, including many prominent folk musicians. On any given weekend night, folk fans might find guitar flat-picker extraordinaire Doc Watson or singer/songwriters John Stewart (ex–Kingston Trio), Tom Waits or Leonard Cohen. On other weekends, the rockers took over. Southern rock legends, like the Outlaws, often played Ebbets, as did Boulder's own electric guitar god, the late Tommy Bolin. Ebbets Field closed its doors in 1982 after serving Denver's music fans for nearly twelve years.

In contrast, the Regency Room at the historic Oxford Hotel presented a less-than-trendy atmosphere in the 1970s. Before its restoration in the late 1990s, the Oxford served primarily as a truckers' hotel in a seedy area of Denver's lower downtown. The Regency Room held perhaps 350 patrons, who sat at rickety tables with mismatched chairs while peering around pillars to view the performers on the small stage, a riser no more than eighteen inches high. The place was noisy, with wait staff bustling about during performances, serving overpriced drinks in the dimly lit room. Still, performances often proved magical—and quite varied. Up-and-coming singer/songwriter Steve Goodman ("The City of New Orleans") killed a capacity crowd in 1978 with his boundless energy and seemingly endless repertoire. Nitty Gritty Dirt Band multi-instrumentalist John McEuen played banjo, guitar and mandolin and invited a visiting Michael Martin Murphy to sit in for a few tunes. Country guitar and mandolin virtuoso Norman Blake awed a quiet and respectful crowd who came to see one of Nashville's most in-demand session players. He did not disappoint. Over the years, in spite of its less-than-glamorous image, the Regency Room proved itself one of Denver's better listening rooms.

The Buckhorn Exchange on Osage Street was, and remains, another kind of club and performance space quite different from others in Denver. The holder of Colorado liquor license number one, this unique Denver landmark utilized folk music to enhance its historic image. Since the 1970s, autoharpist Roz Brown has held sway nearly every Friday and Saturday night in the restaurant's second-floor lounge, crooning cowboy tunes and western folk songs in his unique, unadorned style. Brown started playing on a part-time basis in 1975 and hung out at the Folklore Center. Since 1990, he has made his living playing weekends at the Buckhorn and weekdays at various nursing homes and senior centers and for a variety of civic groups. Brown is a storehouse of folk music, having memorized some four hundred songs. On many weekends, cowboy singer/songwriter Bill Barwick joins Brown at the Buckhorn, lending his lusty baritone and fine guitar playing and offering an astonishing repertoire of modern and traditional tunes.

3

THE DENVER FOLKLORE CENTER

Hal Neustaedter, who died in a private plane crash the very day Tuft arrived back in Denver, had suggested that Harry locate his venture somewhere along Twentieth Avenue, but the places were either too expensive or too far out of the way of traffic flow. Tuft eventually decided on a place on Seventeenth Avenue near Pearl Street, which he rented for fifty-five dollars per month. The district, known as Swallow Hill, lay just east of downtown. The area derived its name not from an unusual presence of feathered creatures but from George R. Swallow, a late nineteenth-century real estate investor. Swallow came to Denver in 1894 and established his law office in the Ernest-Cranmer block on Seventeenth Street, the self-proclaimed "Wall Street of the Rockies." In 1895, he became the president of the Denver Savings Bank at Sixteenth and Arapahoe and began investing in real estate development, his biggest project being the block of East Seventeenth Avenue at Pearl Street.

The brick buildings on the block had seen better days. When Tuft found the space, it was in need of considerable repair, but at least it was affordable. Next door was a restaurant called the Green Spider. In early 1963, as Tuft was unloading building material in front of the store before it opened, he asked a passerby, Larry Shirkey, to give him a hand. "What kind of place will this be?" inquired Shirkey as they unloaded lumber. "A folklore center," replied Tuft. After hearing the explanation of what it was all about, Shirkey, recently graduated from high school, decided that it would be a place worth keeping an eye on. Already bitten by the folk bug after hearing "Tom Dooley," Larry had begun to teach himself five-string

The interior of the original Denver Folklore Center on Seventeenth Avenue. Its comfortable décor always made customers feel at home. *Larry Shirkey.*

The Folklore Center offered instruments, records, books and other musical needs to Denver's growing folk community starting in 1962. *Larry Shirkey.*

banjo. When the store opened for business on March 13, 1962, Larry would be one of Tuft's first customers.

Tuft wanted his place to resemble the New York Folklore Center; he wanted the same rustic, rough-hewn look that made it feel old and antique, like much of the music he favored. He had become friends with George Downing, a high school math teacher, carpenter and former student of architecture at the University of Denver. Tuft wanted knotty pine, but Downing found some inexpensive tongue-in-groove redwood siding, which they used to design the DFC's varied-heights interior, with a walkway between the front and back of the store. The hidden space above the entry walkway provided another necessity: a place where Harry hid his sleeping pallet. What profit the DFC made, Tuft poured back into the store, constantly expanding its stock of records and instruments. He had little left over to live on and for five years used the store as his residence.

GUITAR MAN

The early years proved to be pretty lean. Harry began to search for what MBAs call a revenue stream or lines of business. In addition to his meager opening stock of used instruments, Tuft wanted to add records but had no cash or credit. The 1960s were the days before the now-ubiquitous big box retailers or the Internet. Harry met Austin Miller, who worked for American Records Distributors, run by Joe and Lou Oman, and when Miller visited the store, Harry asked for and received a $200 line of credit. It was not until years later that Tuft learned that Miller, impressed by Tuft's honesty and sincerity, had extended the credit on his own personal guarantee. With his new credit line, Tuft purchased his first batch of one hundred LPs. He also became friends with Maury Samuelson, the proprietor of the Crown Drug Store on California Street, which, at the time, was the only local retailer of Folkways and Elektra records, the two largest and most respected purveyors of noncommercial, non-mainstream folk music. Like Miller, Samuelson extended a small line of credit to the DFC.

But Harry knew that to have any legitimacy in his venture, he had to offer musical instruments, especially guitars, which were gaining daily in popularity. The two biggest names in guitar manufacturing in the United States were C.F. Martin and Gibson. Martin was by far the oldest (established in 1833) and most respected steel-string guitar maker in the world, its handmade

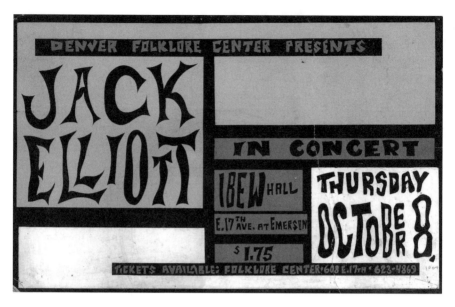

Singer, guitarist and raconteur Ramblin' Jack Elliott, "the last of the Brooklyn cowboys," often appeared in Denver, presented by the Denver Folklore Center.

Harry Tuft presented many of folk music's bigger stars, as well as lesser-known artists like Pete's half brother, the multi-instrumentalist Mike Seeger. Advertising was by handpainted signs. *The Denver Folklore Center.*

instruments played by nearly all the leading folk performers. There were three Martin dealers in the Denver area, all located downtown—Knight-Campbell Music, Wells Music and Happy Logan—and none of them was about to give up this popular but relatively expensive line. Tuft made contact with Coast Wholesale Music in California, which allowed him to purchase Martin guitars for resale. Gibson Guitars of Kalamazoo, Michigan, had no confidence in Tuft's adventure and refused to deal with him at that time, so he made arrangements to carry another brand, Guild Guitars, which came into being in the 1950s after Gibson bought out Epiphone Guitars and absorbed its production into Gibson's Kalamazoo plant. The craftsmen formed the new company and made a name producing good-quality acoustic and electric instruments, and over time the DFC became their leading local dealer. Like a number of others in this burgeoning business, Tuft began to acquire a good understanding of the older-vintage instruments built before World War II. Myths had grown up about the build-quality and tonal characteristics of the prewar Gibson and Martin instruments, and top players sought them out, often paying considerably more for a used 1930s Martin D-28 than a comparable new one. Selling vintage instruments became a specialty business of the Folklore Center.

GOING TO SCHOOL

Martin guitars gave the store certain legitimacy with the local folk crowd, but they hardly made for a substantial cash flow. Even with a stock of instruments, records, books and other musical paraphernalia, something more was needed, something that would create public awareness and bring income to the struggling establishment. Tuft began opening on Sundays to allow for song circles or song-pulls, which became known as hootenannies. The derivation of the term remains unknown, but the dictionary defines hootenanny as "a gathering at which folksingers entertain often with the audience joining in." Players formed a large circle and took turns performing songs, and when appropriate, others joined in on other instruments or harmony vocals. It was a way to make a little cash and share the warmth of the music at the same time. Because of their novelty, the Sunday hoots gave the DFC some much-needed publicity. Still, when Tuft's parents came to visit in the summer of 1962, they were dismayed by the sparseness of the shop. His parents continued to be

Harry Tuft modeled his group guitar lessons on the methods he saw used at the Chicago Old Town School of Folk Music. *Swallow Hill Music Association.*

supportive, but his mother later admitted that she nearly cried when she saw how poor her son's store was.

Even before the store opened its doors, Tuft had been offering group guitar lessons at the Jewish Community Center, and it seemed natural that he should do the same at the new Denver Folklore Center. He began by offering group guitar and banjo lessons on Saturday afternoons. As business improved, Tuft expanded the store into the recently vacated adjacent space, which gave him a chance to enlarge the classes. Using the approach he had observed at the Chicago Old Town School of Folk Music, Tuft had a group of up to eight guitar players with their instructor in one of the store's spaces. Students would learn one to three songs and/or new techniques in their hour-long lesson. At the same time the guitar students were plunking away, a group of banjo students would be learning the same songs in another part of the store. At the end of the hour, the students and instructors gathered for coffee, soft drinks and cookies, milled around and discussed music. After a break, Harry would gather both groups together, and the full ensemble of guitar and banjo students would play the just-learned songs, showing the others what they had mastered and gaining self-confidence in performing with others. On occasion, nationally known musicians would visit, often providing workshops for the more advanced and daring students.

FIRST HIRES

Within the first few weeks of opening, Tuft made a critical personnel decision: he hired Julie Davis to teach guitar. Davis, a student at nearby East High School, was a fifth-generation Coloradan on both sides of her family. A slender girl of medium height with straight blond hair and intense blue eyes, she possessed the long-fingered hands of a musician. She had taken piano lessons in grade school and began to teach herself guitar when she was ten. By fourteen, she was an able guitarist who knew plenty of folk songs, including cowboy tunes learned from her cattle-ranching cousin out on Colorado's eastern plains. She had also picked up other songs from early Joan Baez and Judy Collins records.

Davis was a renegade who didn't fit into the normal high school patterns:

> *I was passionate about music and social issues, especially civil rights. East was quite integrated, and there were many who were openly committed to civil rights. Blacks were moving into our [Park Hill] neighborhood, and my parents said, "Of course, we're going to stay here, and we welcome anyone who comes." Our family's political stance was, "We are completely for civil rights, and we will stand up and work for that." My parents were very active, and I was very active, and it was a time at East that was intense.*

Julie started going to the weekly Sunday jams and played with banjoist Larry Shirkey and guitarist Jack Stanesco:

> *From the beginning it was a gathering of kindred spirits. Even though a lot of us were in high school or college, it was people we couldn't necessarily find at our high school. We were there every Sunday. You just didn't miss one. So there was a community that built up in the Folklore Center's first year. I was one of the younger people at the Folklore Center. I had wanted to take lessons from Harry, but he thought I knew too much since I had taught myself a great deal. So, I couldn't take the beginning lessons or advanced beginning, so he finally let me into an intermediate class, and Harry hired me to teach. So the very first job I ever had, even before I had a driver's license, was teaching guitar at the Folklore Center.*

Tuft taught group lessons on Wednesday evenings and Saturday afternoons. Davis remembered, "So I would come on Saturday and take the beginning guitar class, then turn around and teach it the following

Group lessons at the DFC and now at Swallow Hill are exciting and fun, just the way homegrown music should be. *Swallow Hill Music Association.*

Wednesday evening. We would cycle through, and I would teach the beginning, then advanced class." Davis claims that she learned an important lesson from both her piano teacher and Tuft, her two models of teaching: it's about the student, not you; you watch them grow. For a while, she was the only guitar teacher Tuft hired. Later, he added Ray Chatfield to teach banjo and Matt Ferris to teach mandolin. That trio formed the core of the DFC faculty for some time. "The whole idea was empowering people, getting them out there with their guitars and letting them play."

And it was more than the music. Davis recalled:

It was absolutely special and magical. I felt that I had a place where not only I could express myself, but I could learn from other people who were older than me. For example, Phyllis Wagner was in philosophy at DU, and Bart was in graduate school. Just listening to them talk, engaging them in conversation, I felt I was learning so much about the social movements, about life, about things that people who were curious were paying attention to. But because they were so much older, they were bringing experience to it that I didn't have.

There's Something Happening Here

Social issues have always been important in folk music, and the 1960s proved to be a time of flowering for songs of social comment. The Vietnam War had not yet escalated into the televised horror it would become, but nightly news carried pictures of the civil rights struggle from places like Birmingham and Little Rock. Music played an important role in the civil rights movement, whose leaders used it to unite and energize, as well as to calm fears when confronted with blatant hatred. At lunch counter sit-ins, protest marches and church meetings, singing became a bond that buoyed flagging spirits and calmed fears. The civil rights movement was born in the southern churches, so rich with musical history, and in time, folk and gospel music intertwined and created the movement's best-known and loved songs: "We Shall Overcome," "Keep Your Eyes on the Prize" and "We Shall Not Be Moved."

The folk music community, always sensitive to human rights issues and its roots deep in the New Left, embraced the movement. Singers like Pete Seeger and Joan Baez donated their time and talents, marching with protesters and leading crowds in song. Later, Peter, Paul and Mary and Bob Dylan sang and wrote about the struggle. For Julie Davis—and others, one suspects—the Folklore Center was an extension of the music and social ideals.

"Harry, Phyllis and I talked about civil rights and other movements all the time. They were the subjects that brought people together," recalled Davis.

It was a time when records were coming out from all over the world. We talked about other cultures, the mores of other people, about political systems, about politics all around the world. And we talked very definitely about the politics and what was going on with the civil rights movement, and the folk music movement and the whole emerging network of communications around the country. As Harry got into concert promotions, even before he had the concert hall, and he produced concerts and there was a steady stream of people that were coming through who were at the forefront of the Civil Rights and Folk Movements. So we had Peter, Paul and Mary, we had Josh White. All these people talking about what was going on in Washington and elsewhere. And it was what Phyllis and I would talk about when we were working the counter.

Community means many things to many people, but there has been a special bond in the folk community that extends beyond the camaraderie of the music itself. In the 1960s, the Folklore Center provided a home away from home for visiting musicians and patrons alike. Tragedy sometimes illustrates the communal bond. Davis recalled:

I remember where I was when I heard about Kennedy. I was in Spanish class, and the teacher—everybody was devastated. We were sitting there when we first heard he was shot, and then somebody came door to door and said he had died. The school reacted. I mean, for so many of us, well, I came from a liberal Republican family, not a conservative, an old-style liberal Republican family, but I had been very hopeful about Kennedy. And the school seemed to be of one heart and mind and soul when that happened. Here we were, an integrated school, about a third of us were white, a third black, and a third that was everything else under the sun. And here was someone who we felt was trying to create a model for all of this to work.

And so, I actually left from the school and went to the Folklore Center, as did a lot of us. It was where we gathered. Vince deFrancis, Jack Stanesco, Larry Shirkey. A lot of us that went to the Folklore Center. The mood was somber, very somber, just sitting there trying to comprehend. Of course, it turned out to be just the first of a long string of assassinations. There was very little speaking. There wasn't a TV on; there wasn't a radio on; at that point it was just being together. It just felt like the right place to be. It was a gathering place for many people for days afterward.

R-E-S-P-E-C-T

As business grew and his reputation in the folk community solidified, Tuft saw more opportunities to grow. When the Green Spider closed in 1967, Tuft expanded the DFC into its vacated space. His enterprises eventually occupied 600–14 Seventeenth Avenue, more than half the block along the busy thoroughfare. Feeling rather good about his success, he approached guitar maker C.F. Martin and Company, saying, "I've been selling Martin guitars for a few years. Would you allow me to deal with you direct?" This time they agreed.

Key to the success would be accomplished bluegrass guitar and banjo player the late David Ferretta, who passed away at the age of forty-seven in 1994. A committed conscientious objector, in 1963 Ferretta came to Denver, where he completed his alternative service at the offices of the American Friends Service Committee on Pennsylvania Street, near Colfax Avenue. Ferretta was up front with Harry from the beginning, telling him that it was his intention to open his own shop within three years, and if that precluded him from consideration for a job at the DFC, so be it. Tuft was not concerned; he hired Ferretta.

According to the contract between Martin Guitars and the store, the Folklore Center would place an order for instruments every six months, paying half the bill when placing the order and the remainder upon delivery. Harry recalled, "I'd get the order form and give it to David to fill out. When I got it back, I'd say, 'David, how are we going to pay for these guitars?' He'd answer, 'Don't worry; we'll sell 'em.' What he really meant was, 'I'll sell them.' And he did. He really built the store." Pete Wernick, banjoist for the band Hot Rize, said, "He went out of his way to make a customer and a friend." The DFC eventually became the largest Martin dealer between Chicago and Salt Lake City, and Ferretta went on to open his own shop (Ferretta's Global Village, on South Pennsylvania), which he patterned on the Folklore Center.

Because of his connections with many leading performers from his time in New York and Philadelphia, and Denver's convenient location on the way to and from the West Coast, Tuft began to promote performances. How did a young entrepreneur, with no promotion experience, reputation or cash, get started? It was mostly a case of being in the right place at the right time. The promotion business at the time was considerably simpler and less legally bound up than it is in the twenty-first century. It often began when a visiting artist stopped in at the store and Tuft asked him or her to conduct a workshop.

Larry Shirkey recalls Tuft talking with Taj Mahal, the then Boston-based blues/folk artist, who had stopped off in Denver on his way to Los Angeles. Harry asked Taj if he would consider giving a concert. Taj answered, "Sure. Where?" "How about right here?" In a matter of a few days, word spread quickly that the DFC would host the talented Taj Mahal in concert. He used the performance space next to the store where the DFC hosted hoots and open-microphone nights. The show was a sellout.

Because of Denver's growing reputation in folk music circles as a great place to play, in no small part because of the DFC, Tuft received a call in March 1964 from Manny Greenhill, Joan Baez's manager. Greenhill was well regarded in the entertainment business and considered a member of the "folk mafia," a group that included Albert Grossman, manager of Bob Dylan, Pete Seeger and Peter, Paul and Mary. They had earned the sobriquet not so much for a predilection toward violence and dark acts but rather for their managerial control over folk music's most successful acts and of the Newport Folk Festival. Tuft's name and the Folklore Center's reputation had spread in the world of folk music primarily through their mention in articles and columns in *Sing Out!*, widely recognized as the official magazine of the folk movement. Greenhill wanted Tuft to promote Baez's first-ever Denver show. In 1964, Baez was regarded as the reigning queen of folk music and was at the top of her career. Tuft had none of the needed experience and resisted Greenhill's initial request, claiming that he had neither the background nor the money to promote Baez's show. Greenhill countered, saying that he would take care of all the expenses and would give Tuft 10 percent of the show's gross. He added, "I'll walk you through promoting." They struck an agreement, and the show sold out weeks in advance.

Joan Baez arrived in Denver on the train. Alone. She had no entourage or handlers, and Tuft picked her up at Union Station. Greenhill arrived a few days before the show to help make final arrangements, and Baez delivered an outstanding performance. The day after the show, Tuft took Joan to Red Rocks to show her Denver's famous outdoor amphitheater.

The DFC presented Joan Baez in concert at Red Rocks Amphitheater for the first time, just weeks before the Beatles invaded the Rocks on their landmark 1964 American tour. Music changed forever after the British Invasion. *Larry Shirkey.*

Situated near the town of Morrison about fifteen miles from downtown Denver, Red Rocks is a geological wonder. Its story dates to the creation of the Fountain Formation, sedimentary rocks that eroded from the ancestral Rocky Mountains some 300 million years ago. As a way to preserve and protect the site's unique geology, Denver acquired the 640 acres in 1928 to create one of its thirteen Denver Mountain Parks. George E. Cranmer, then head of the Denver Parks and Improvements Department under Mayor Benjamin F. Stapleton, was impressed by the site's natural acoustics. Having enjoyed a play at an amphitheater while visiting Italy, Cranmer believed Denver could create an outdoor stage in this unique setting.

The city hired noted architect Burnham Hoyt to handle the design. Hoyt's challenge was to create an amphitheater, with its stage, dressing rooms and seating, while making minimum impact on the physical beauty and structure of the 440-foot-tall red rock spires. His design shaped the

The Folklore Center presented numerous shows in the 1960s, including one by popular Canadian duo Ian & Sylvia. *The Denver Folklore Center.*

seating and architecture to fit the site rather than molding the site to fit a plan. He succeeded. Cranmer convinced the federal Works Progress Administration (WPA) to build the roads and parking lots. Between 1935 and 1941, the federal Civilian Conservation Corps (CCC) put hundreds of seventeen- to twenty-five-year-olds to work constructing the park and amphitheater. With seating for 9,400, Red Rocks is the only naturally occurring amphitheater in the world.

In 1969, the Denver Folklore Center presented Arlo Guthrie (standing) and Pete Seeger in their first-ever public performance together. They would go on to be a popular pairing for many years. *Larry Shirkey.*

Tuft and Baez strolled around the facility and walked onto the stage, where they performed an impromptu drama to an empty amphitheater. Tuft had been quietly urging Baez to perform there. Seeing the place convinced her it would work, but what really cemented the deal was when Baez learned that the Beatles, then the hottest music act in America, were scheduled to play the Rocks on their first U.S. tour. That summer, Harry Tuft presented Joan Baez in a successful show at Red Rocks. A week later, Joan returned to Denver and got her wish: she met John, Paul, George and Ringo for the first time.

It all sounds rather glamorous in retrospect, but the promotion and music business was much less pretentious in the days before the Woodstock Festival and arena rock shows. Once Greenhill had mentored Tuft, he expected reciprocity. A short time later, Greenhill called and said, "It's pretty short notice, but I want you to do something for me. Now that I've made you a lot of money, I want you to do a concert with Jim Kweskin and the Jug Band at Phipps Auditorium." Tuft knew the band and had met Kweskin and singer Geoff Muldaur, but the band was not exactly a household name in Denver. The week before the Denver date, the band appeared on *The Steve Allen Show*, one of the most popular shows on television. But promotion was often hit or miss, and Kweskin's group sold just 350 of the 900 seats at Phipps. Through the 1960s and early '70s, Tuft promoted a few big-name artists at Red Rocks, including the successful first-ever pairing of Pete Seeger and Arlo Guthrie in 1969. Tuft focused most of his performance promotion on smaller shows at the DFC, including performances by Judy Collins, Jack Elliott and guitar great Doc Watson. He promoted local acts, such as the City Limits Bluegrass Band and the Rambling Drifters, who would one day morph into the successful bluegrass group Hot Rize. Jazz/country guitar great Bill Frisell took some of his first guitar lessons from Bob Marcus at the Folklore Center and remembers it as "a fantastic music store, record shop, concert hall and meeting place for musicians."

WIDER HORIZONS

To publicize the store, Tuft devised what might be the first comprehensive "folk source" catalogue. Working with Phyllis Wagner (now Phyllis Jane Rose), they produced "The Denver Folklore Center Catalog and Almanac of Folk Music," which combined a mail-order catalogue with a compendium of information regarding the developing folk movement, such as listings of

Impromptu picking sessions were common at the DFC. Seen here in the late 1960s are (from left) a banjo player (unknown), David Ferretta, a fiddle player (unknown), Harry Tuft, Wesley Westbrooks and Dick Weissman. *Larry Shirkey.*

stores, manufacturers and music festivals. Tuft had one thousand copies printed, but how to market them? How could he reach the national folk community? He reckoned that the 1965 Newport Folk Festival might give him the reach he sought.

The Newport Folk Festival grew out of the successful jazz festival held at the posh seaside resort. First held in 1959, it had grown into the largest festival of its kind and featured performers from every possible corner of the folk spectrum. Acts included string bands from the Appalachian Mountains and Delta and country blues (Mississippi John Hurt and Fred McDowell), as well as the more rock-like urban blues from Chicago (Paul Butterfield Blues Band), bluegrass and gospel (the Stanley Brothers, Bill Monroe and the Bluegrass Boys) and an assortment of the best the urban folk revival had to offer (Phil Ochs; Peter, Paul and Mary; Bob Dylan). The festival drew large crowds over a four-day weekend run—175 performers in six concerts and twenty-six workshops. The 1965 festival, however, was most noted for Dylan's first public foray in the electric world of rock-and-roll, when he performed a short set backed by Butterfield's blistering band. It shook the folk world to its core.

Earth-shattering or not, it seemed like a good marketing venue. Tuft's catalogue, the first of its kind to draw so many "folk sources" together, drew praise from everyone. It bestowed on Tuft and the Folklore Center something of a national reputation among folk musicians and fans. Oddly, Tuft did not exploit his marketing success or move to expand aggressively into mail-order marketing, but Stan Werblin saw the genius of the effort. Attending Newport that year, he purchased one of Harry's catalogues and exploited the idea. He eventually founded Elderly Music in Lansing, Michigan, developing it into one of the largest and most successful catalogue and Internet instrument and music suppliers.

CALIFORNIA DREAMIN'

Harry spent most days at the store talking to customers, scheduling classes and trying to stay out of debt. The store's relaxed atmosphere attracted a wide variety of people, and not just musicians. A young lawyer, Richard Lamm, known as Dick to his friends, often visited during his lunch hour, walking up from his offices in the Petroleum Building at Broadway and Sixteenth Street. Lamm does not recall how he and Tuft first met or how he became aware of the DFC, but he "regarded it as a place of refuge. I was a very high-tension young man, over-committed, and I used the Denver Folklore Center as a place to relax and meet real people. I used to go there and just sit. I attended many of their concerts and would love to just go and talk with Harry, a real human being in a world of self-important people." The store had that kind of effect on the many people who made up the DFC community.

Tuft never considered himself a true political activist, but Lamm, then head of the Young Democrats, drew him into that organization and asked him to help organize political events, such as the "Bury Goldwater Hootenanny" and the "Goldwater Hate-In." Tuft rented out a place, brought in a jug band and a gospel group and sold out the four-hundred-seat hall.

Following the successful Baez promotion, 1966 brought an unanticipated opportunity. Harry received a phone call from the manager of the Mamas and the Papas, whose leader, John Phillips, was Dick Weissman's old band mate from the Journeymen. The Mamas and the Papas, with their exceptional

Phillips vocal arrangements, had an unexpected smash hit with their first release, "California Dreamin'." While it wasn't exactly "folk music," they needed a promoter for their upcoming Denver show at the Auditorium Arena, but in order to promote the show, Harry needed to come up with a $5,000 guarantee, the kind of money he simply did not have. He talked about it with Lamm during one of the lawyer's lunchtime visits, and Lamm agreed to become Tuft's partner for the show and fronted the guarantee.

While not showing it at the time, Lamm was clearly nervous about the arrangement. The way Lamm remembered it, "Harry asked me to cosign a loan, one thing young lawyers should never do. But I did, and it looked like we were going to lose money until the week before the concert. The Mamas and Papas appeared on the cover of *Time* magazine." The *Time* cover was the result of the group's phenomenal popularity. Tuft recalled, "And suddenly he relaxed. Anyway, we sold the concert out. And I fondly remember giving him two bags full of money to take up to what

SATURDAY OCT. 8
8 P.M. AUDITORIUM ARENA
13TH AND CHAMPA

KIMN and the **HIPBONE**
PRESENT

THE MAMAS & THE PAPAS

PLUS
THE BENZIE KRYCK
THE "NEW" MOONRAKERS
THE RAINY DAZE

TICKETS ON SALE HERE
ORCHESTRA 3.50   MEZZANINE 3.00   GENERAL ADMISSION BALCONY 2.50
HIPBONE   715 16th STREET   GATEWAY MUSIC - AURORA
DENVER FOLKLORE CENTER   608 E. 17th AVE.   JERRY'S BRIAR & BOOKS
RECORD CENTER   434 16th STREET   2016 SO. UNIV., D. U.
ALL HOWELL DEPARTMENT STORES   ALLEGRO MUSIC - CHERRY CREEK
ENGLEWOOD MEN'S STORE   BROOMFIELD BANK
FRIENDLY DRUG 5660 W. ALAMEDA   BLUE JAY - BOULDER
MAN'S WORLD - LITTLETON   HOLIDAY ON THE HILL - BOULDER
BALL MUSIC - LAKESIDE   VOICE & VISION   5705 E. COLFAX

Though not exactly considered folk music at the time, Harry Tuft and future Colorado governor Richard Lamm teamed up to present the Mamas and the Papas in a sold-out show at Denver's Auditorium Arena in 1965. *The Denver Folklore Center.*

was then the Denver National Bank's night deposit box with a police escort, with $17,000 out of a total gross of $22,000. It was a sellout, 6,700 attendees. And Dick took his half of the money and ran his first campaign for the Colorado House of Representatives." Lamm went on to become a two-term Colorado governor. The whole idea of it all tickled John Phillips, who would later joke that he was a king maker, that he had helped make Lamm governor of Colorado.

Concert promotion aside, Lamm and Tuft became friends. Tuft says:

> I don't know if you've met him, or if you know much about him, but he's naturally one of the most charismatic people I have ever met. He just has a wonderful way about him, and I enjoyed his company. And he was very generous, included me in his social world, and I went on hikes with his family. I was alone at the time and didn't know anything about the mountains or climbing. His brother Tom came out to Denver, and Tom became my lawyer. With Tom, I did a bunch of technical climbing.

Often together, Lamm and Tuft organized and performed at fundraisers and anti-war protests and supported other liberal causes throughout the 1960s and into the '70s. While Harry never considered himself a proselytizer, he kept songs with a social message as part of his repertoire and appeared at concerts advocating peace and social justice.

HIPPIE LEADER

By the end of the '60s, the DFC had gained a reputation as a "hippie hangout," at least in the eyes of conservative people. The store's location on Seventeenth Avenue placed it squarely among coffeehouses like La Petite Café and youth-oriented organizations like the Hip Help Center at Seventeenth and Ogden, run by Joe Arnold. Tuft remembered getting calls from parents who could not understand what was happening to their children. "In general in the community, we were considered a good store, although some parents were sometimes afraid to let their kids go down there for lessons, not so much to the store but to the area." It was a time when parents had difficulty understanding their children, when popular music seemed more alien than ever and drugs seemed to be everywhere. On the other hand, some parents perceived Tuft and the Folklore Center as a bridge

A youthful Harry Tuft sometime in the late 1960s. He is sitting in front of the Denver Folklore Center with a borrowed dog and guitar. *The Denver Folklore Center.*

between them and their children. "These were folks with 1940s/'50s values of home and family, and here were these kids that were just totally different. They just couldn't understand."

Not everyone thought well of the DFC. The *Rocky Mountain News* published a story in the late 1960s about the people who owned businesses along East

Seventeenth Avenue, including Tuft and the owners of the neighboring Third Eye Theater and Green Spider nightclub. The story included a picture of the business owners with a caption calling them "Hippie Leaders," as if there were some kind of organized movement. In their concern to clean up some of the drugs on the street, detectives at the Denver Police Department decided to make an example of one of those leaders. An anonymous caller, apparently from the DA's office, informed Tuft of the detectives' intent. Tuft, while appreciating the concern, had never had a taste or tolerance for drugs and considered the plan silly, knowing he had nothing to hide. Still, for a time he noticed mysterious clicks on his phone line every time he used it. Nothing more came of it.

In the late 1960s and early 1970s, Tuft continued selling instruments and presenting concerts at his Seventeenth Avenue facility, as well as at other Denver venues. Having had success with Joan Baez concerts, Tuft sought to bring hometown girl Judy Collins back to Denver.

JUDY COLLINS

The young Judy Collins had graduated from East High School and studied with the famed classical pianist and conductor Dr. Antonia Brico. Collins, like so many others, had been smitten with the purity and beauty of traditional folk music, especially the Weavers. While still in high school, she added the guitar to her instrumental repertoire. She performed in school productions and impressed Neustaedter enough that he offered her $150 a week for an extended engagement. She eventually decided to relocate to New York City to further her career but often returned to Denver to perform as she gained national acclaim.

Judy Collins was Denver's own folk-singing daughter. She was born on May 1, 1939, in Seattle, Washington, and from the time she was a toddler demonstrated an ability to carry a tune. Her father, Charles Thomas Collins, was born in Idaho and, due to a birth trauma, was completely blind by age four. The elder Collins graduated from the University of Idaho, where he led a dance band with his sweet Irish tenor. After college, he began his radio career at KOMO in Seattle.

Charles Collins took a job in Denver in 1949, when Judy was ten. He hosted a popular radio program each day at 10:15 a.m. called *Chuck Collins Calling*, where he sang songs, read poetry and philosophized. Judy

A relic from the 1960s: a program cover from a Judy Collins concert presented by the Denver Friends of Folk Music. *Swallow Hill Music Association.*

had begun piano lessons a few years earlier and showed considerable promise, but shortly after moving to Denver, she learned she had polio. Remarkably, she recovered, but only after a long stay in the hospital. After her recovery, she reinitiated her study of the piano and auditioned for the famous Dr. Antonia Brico, the first woman to conduct a symphony orchestra in America. Judy passed her audition, and while she worked hard, Brico, who thought Collins had considerable talent, complained that she did not practice nearly enough.

There were other musical influences in her life. Like many youngsters, Collins had learned the pop songs of the day from radio and Irish ballads from her father. The elder Collins invited his daughter to play piano and sing on his radio show, and Judy's performance career was underway. She appeared regularly and met many of the celebrities who appeared on the show.

Collins attended East High School, where she often performed in school programs with two of her classmates in a group called the Little Reds. It was while she was in high school that Collins heard her first folk song. Jo Stafford's version of "Barbara Allen" entranced her; the emotion of the lyrics was like nothing she had heard before. Sensing that piano was not the instrument of choice for folk music, she badgered her father into getting her a guitar and taught herself to play.

In 1956, when she was sixteen, she met Lingo the Drifter, who hosted an all–folk music radio program on Saturday afternoons that Collins and her father listened to frequently. It was from Lingo that Collins learned not only a bit more about guitar accompaniment but also about songs with political themes, the songs of Woody Guthrie and Cisco Houston.

After graduating from Denver East High School, Collins auditioned at Michael's Pub in Boulder in 1959. Even though the owner claimed to hate folk music, the crowd loved her. The owner knew a good thing and invited her back for an extended stay, and from then on Michael's was known as a folk club. Her success at Michael's led to her first appearance at the Exodus, where, during an extended engagement, she opened for notable folk acts such as the Tarriers (one of the first integrated folk groups) and Bob Gibson. Her Exodus appearances and other shows around Colorado gave her the courage to expand her horizons, and she was invited to appear in April at the Gate of Horn in Chicago, where she received good reviews and lots of exposure. In 1961, Collins realized that if she were to advance her career, she would have to relocate to New York, the acknowledged center of the folk universe. She made the move and soon began appearing at Gerde's Folk City on West Fourth Street in Greenwich Village. There she met another Village newcomer, Bob Dylan, who had arrived a few months earlier and was just beginning to try his hand at writing new material. That same year, she met Jac Holtzman, the owner of Elektra Records, then a small privately owned folk-oriented record label. Holtzman liked what he heard and encouraged Collins to record her first album. While not wildly successful, the critics enjoyed it, and her recording career was on its way.

By 1965, Collins had clearly established herself as one of the leading female folk vocalists. Her appearance on *Hootenanny* had given her wider exposure, and her albums were gaining larger audiences. In the 1960s, Collins returned to Denver to visit family and perform. Harry Tuft booked Collins a number of times, but one appearance stood out in his mind. In town for Christmas with her family, Collins joined Tuft and a group of local folkies for a private Christmas party at the Denver Folklore Center, where they all took turns playing.

Collins went on to greater fame and much wider recognition. After introducing the world to the songs of Joni Mitchell and Leonard Cohen through her album *Wildflowers*, she scored a big hit with her cover of Ian Tyson's "Someday Soon." She followed that up with a most unlikely hit: her haunting version of "Amazing Grace," with bagpipe accompaniment.

HARD TIMES COME AGAIN NO MORE

The Folklore Center had gained the well-deserved reputation as Denver's home for folk and acoustic music, but business was changing. The popularity of folk-style music declined sharply in the late 1970s as bubble gum rock-and-roll and disco dominated popular music, and it became increasingly difficult to keep the store profitable. With the shift in musical tastes and the economic recession, acoustic guitar sales fell perceptibly. C.F. Martin's annual instrument production plummeted from a high of 22,637 guitars in 1971 to just 3,153 guitars in 1982. The DFC struggled with fewer customers and fewer students. Tuft contemplated closing the store.

At the end of 1978, Tuft totaled up the year's expenses and revenue and discovered that the concert hall had lost $15,000. The concerts provided good advertising for the DFC, but it was hard to justify that level of expense. Tuft sat down with a few of his longtime Denver friends, including Jeff Withers, Alan Kelly and Larry Shirkey, to discuss the option of creating a nonprofit organization to run concert promotions. As a nonprofit, the group would be able to apply for grants and would have fewer tax burdens while relieving the DFC of the expenses. The group agreed to the idea but then discovered that in order to qualify as a nonprofit, it would need to offer educational services. Tuft responded by agreeing to turn over the music classes that had been a central part of the Folklore Center since its inception and provide space at no charge. The group cast about for a name and created the Music Association of Swallow Hill (MASH). It seemed like a good arrangement for everyone, and Swallow Hill had little trouble at the beginning, presenting shows at the DFC's concert space, as well as at a number of locations around Denver, and expanding school operations.

Then Tuft learned that he had lost the lease on the Seventeenth Avenue properties when the owners decided to sell out to developers wanting to construct a 7-11 convenience store on the site. Tuft and Swallow Hill had few options. In March 1980, Tuft closed the store.

But not everyone was willing to see it all go away. The DFC's repair shop manager, Rick Kirby, convinced Tuft to sell out to him, taking the name and most of the store's stock and reestablishing the Denver Folklore Center on South Broadway. The building was a converted house, and Swallow Hill was able to rent the rooms on the second floor, converting them into classrooms for music lessons.

Tuft was relieved to be able to do other things with his life. He had put nearly all his time and energy into the DFC for nearly seventeen years, and it was time for a change. He continued to give guitar lessons and perform occasionally and served for a time on Swallow Hill's board of directors. His friend state treasurer Sam Brown had just purchased the BMH Synagogue building at Sixteenth and Gaylord and asked Tuft to convert it into a performance space and manage it. Swallow Hill and others presented shows there, but the project never made money. Tuft continued acting as Brown's closing manager for low-income housing projects and developed condominium associations. In 1989, the Denver Musicians Union hired Tuft as executive director, and he remained in this post until 1991, when the union's new president wanted to reestablish the traditional union infrastructures of president, vice-president and secretary.

The economic recession overtook Rick Kirby and the relocated Folklore Center. In 1983, Tuft briefly returned to the store and paid off all outstanding debts, even though he was not personally responsible for them, thus keeping the name of the Folklore Center in good standing with its creditors. Then he closed the Folklore Center's doors for good. Or so he thought.

4

SWALLOW HILL MUSIC ASSOCIATION

Stayin' Alive

The beginning of the 1970s saw significant change in America. The "Summer of Love" and the hippie era came to a crashing close. America agonized over its involvement in the Vietnam War; it was President Lyndon Johnson's downfall. President Richard Nixon resigned in disgrace. Musical tastes and economic fortunes changed considerably, and acoustic music in general—and folk music in particular—was in recession. The Top 40 and album-oriented AM and FM radio stations played an increasingly homogenized mix of music, dominated by dance, disco and bubble gum (a derisive term that described sweet, mindless Top 40 pop). Punk—a new, edgier and rebellious music—was beginning to percolate just beneath the pop mainstream. Folk acts popular in the 1960s (the Kingston Trio; Peter, Paul and Mary; Ian and Sylvia; the Highwaymen; the Brothers Four) disappeared from the popular stage, disbanding, with their members often retreating to the corporate world. Folk music was simply not hip. In the days before widespread cable television, fans of folk and country music were left with few choices, a notable exception being *Austin City Limits* on PBS, which often offered non-mainstream country acts like Waylon Jennings and Willie Nelson and singer/songwriters, including John Prine and Steve Goodman.

Arguably, folk music had never been truly hip; its commercial boom in the late 1950s and early '60s—what some participants, like Tom Rush and James Taylor, with their tongues firmly planted in their cheeks, refer to as the "Folk Scare"—registered only marginally on the national scene. If Billboard #1 Hits are any indication, folk music was a breeze, not a hurricane. The Kingston Trio's "Tom Dooley" reached the number one position in November 1958, but no other folk group was able to duplicate that feat until September 1961, when the Highwaymen put "Michael Row the Boat Ashore" on top of the charts. The Rooftop Singers followed in January 1963 ("Walk Right In"), but that was it. A reasonable number of folk acts—including Peter, Paul and Mary; the New Christy Minstrels; and the Brothers Four—charted Top Ten records during the early 1960s, but none cracked the top spot. Peter, Paul and Mary finally got a number one in 1969 with their cover of John Denver's "Leaving on a Jet Plane."

Folk music was just popular enough to generate some interest from the television networks. ABC television broadcast *Hootenanny* for a season and a half in 1963–64. Set on college campuses and hosted by Jack Linkletter, the program showcased established and up-and-coming folk acts, from a very young Judy Collins and Ian and Sylvia, to commercial (and often cookie-cutter) groups like the Back Porch Majority, the Limelighters and Brothers Four, to traditional acts such as Flatt and Scruggs and the Carter Family. *Hootenanny* was far from daring, and its producers assiduously avoided the young, controversial, often angry protest singers like Tom Paxton and Phil Ochs. Paxton's pro-labor "The High Sheriff of Hazard" ("Now the High Sheriff of Hazard is a hardworking man / To be a fine sheriff is his only plan / With his hands in our pockets he takes what he can / For he's the High Sheriff of Hazard.") and Ochs's anti-war "I Ain't Marchin' Anymore" ("Oh I marched to the Battle of New Orleans / At the end of the early British war / The young land started growing / The young blood started flowing / But I ain't marchin' anymore.") did not endear them to the show's producers, who blacklisted Pete Seeger. Other artists, notably Joan Baez and Bob Dylan, stood on principle and refused to appear on *Hootenanny*.

Television was not the only media to avoid the controversy of protest singers. Radio gave no airplay to the brewing storm. The 1960s witnessed the rise of the topical singer, and after Bob Dylan began his climb to stardom, others followed in his early protest singer mold. Young, angry writers took to the stage and recording studio to comment on civil rights, labor conflict and the vagaries of nuclear war. The best of them (early Bob Dylan, Phil Ochs, Richard Fariña and Tom Paxton) were more than protest singers, to be sure, but made their initial marks writing about controversial subjects. Only Dylan flirted with runaway success, charting two number two hits in 1965, though the Byrds' folk-rock cover of his "Mr. Tambourine Man" made it to the top spot that year. "Blowin' in the Wind" and "The Eve of Destruction" were among the few topical songs to make it into the Top 40.

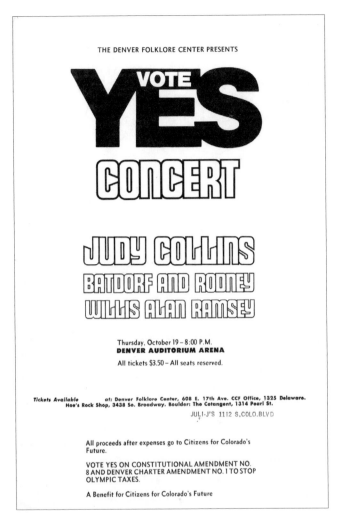

THE DENVER FOLKLORE CENTER PRESENTS

VOTE YES CONCERT

JUDY COLLINS
BATDORF AND RODNEY
WILLIS ALAN RAMSEY

Thursday, October 19 – 8:00 P.M.
DENVER AUDITORIUM ARENA
All tickets $3.50 – All seats reserved.

Tickets Available   at: Denver Folklore Center, 608 E. 17th Ave. CCF Office, 1325 Delaware.
Hoo's Rock Shop, 3438 So. Broadway. Boulder: The Cotangent, 1314 Pearl St.
JULI-J'S 1112 S.COLO.BLVD

All proceeds after expenses go to Citizens for Colorado's Future.

VOTE YES ON CONSTITUTIONAL AMENDMENT NO. 8 AND DENVER CHARTER AMENDMENT NO. 1 TO STOP OLYMPIC TAXES.

A Benefit for Citizens for Colorado's Future

While not overtly political himself, Harry Tuft, often with encouragement from Dick Lamm, presented artists in shows in support of political causes, this one to stop Colorado from hosting the Olympic Games. *The Denver Folklore Center.*

There had been just three folk music number one hits by the time the Beatles swept into American popular music in February 1964, when they twice appeared on the popular variety program *The Ed Sullivan Show.* By the summer, the Beatles dominated the charts, having seven of the top ten singles at one time, and led the so-called British Invasion. The subsequent shift in popular tastes more or less killed folk music, at least as the center of popular culture.

Folk and acoustic music in its many forms—string bands, old-timey, bluegrass, new age, blues and especially singer/songwriters—soldiered on through the '60s and into the '70s but never regained the center of attention either nationally or locally. Harry Tuft continued to present music of all folk forms at the Denver Folklore Center, as did other local venues—Ebetts Field, Sweet Loretta's, the Regency Room at the Oxford Hotel, the Exodus, Café York, the Green Spider and the Satire Lounge. All had bustled in the 1960s and early '70s but either shifted their presentations to other, more popular musical forms or went out of business entirely.

OUT OF THE EGG

On Monday, November 13, 1978, a crowd of some thirty to forty hardcore folk music fans gathered at the Folklore Center's concert hall. They weren't there to play or listen to music; instead, they heard Harry explain that his concert series had lost more than $10,000 the previous year and had been oozing cash for the past five years. The rest of the Folklore Center—the music school, instrument sales, repair shop and bead shop—was apparently fiscally sound. As much as anyone, Harry was reluctant to simply end concert promotion at the DFC, and he sought the input of his loyal customers.

A series of meetings of concerned patrons ensued, and several ideas for saving the concert hall emerged. The best scheme, an idea Harry supported, seemed to be the formation of a nonprofit, community-supported organization that would operate independently from the Folklore Center. After some investigation, however, it became clear that to qualify for nonprofit tax status, the organization had to include an educational component. Harry not only offered the organizers the concert hall rent-free but also agreed to turn over the school of his business. With the school in the mix, advocates grew excited about the possibilities, throwing out ideas for music workshops, songwriting showcases and a grant-supported concert series. Alan Kelly, then the concert hall manager, suggested that remodeling the hall and getting a liquor license might add to the bottom line. The organizers finally agreed that a nonprofit focusing on education and concert promotion was the best avenue.

In February 1979, the group elected its first board of directors. Geoff Withers would serve as president, while Roz Brown, Emmie Hewitt, Bill McCreary, Tom McMillan, Elissa Meyer and Larry Shirkey made up the board. The group deliberated over a name. Hitting on the idea of combining the name of the Swallow Hill neighborhood, music and the influence of a

A group of passionate individuals came together to form the Music Association of Swallow Hill when Harry Tuft was forced to close the original Denver Folklore Center on Seventeenth Avenue. *Swallow Hill Music Association.*

hit television show, the board dubbed the new organization MASH—the Music Association of Swallow Hill.

Tuft officially closed the Folklore Center concert hall on March 1, 1979, and turned its operation over to the fledgling MASH. The young organization celebrated its new beginnings with a three-day benefit concert on March 16–18. The performers included Harry Tuft, Rich Moore, Steve Stajich, Dan McCrimmon, the Rambling Drifters (soon to be Hot Rize), Kathy deFrancis, Roz Brown & Friends, Jaime Brockett, David Ferretta & the Sunday River Boys, Greg Price, Larry Sandberg, Alan Kelly, Michael Stanwood, Sweet Georgia Brown and Generic Bluegrass. The *Rocky Mountain News*, on March 31, 1979, noted, "The transition has been a seamless one. Swallow Hillians, now eighty strong, want no radical change but seem content with the mellow coffee-house format." MASH retained Alan Kelly as concert manager.

The concert was a success, but the road remained rocky for years to come. More than once Swallow Hill teetered on the brink of extinction as money and organizational problems plagued the association. When the Denver Folklore Center relocated to 440 South Broadway, Swallow Hill followed. The building was an old two-story house with a storefront tacked on. The DFC music shop and store occupied the street level; Swallow Hill subleased the upper floor from the Folklore Center, where it set up its school and office space. It wasn't much—just three lesson rooms, an office and restrooms. Less than a year after moving, developers razed the old Denver Folklore Center building on Seventeenth Avenue and built a 7-11 convenience store.

MOVIN' ON

But the overall condition of the Denver folk music scene was far from rosy. MASH had just 143 members and no competition after David Ferretta's Global Village had closed the previous December, leaving MASH as the last venue specializing in folk music. Ever the optimist, Harry Tuft told the *Denver Magazine*, "I wouldn't say the future of folk music here is bleak. Tentative or vague or fragile, maybe, but not bleak." Vintage Harry Tuft.

Tentative or bleak, Swallow Hill struggled. There was no shortage of ideas—some rather grandiose—but no one seemed to be able to create funding for any of them. The school was moderately successful; at least it broke even. To celebrate the move to South Broadway, MASH planned a lively concert series at the now-defunct West Auditorium in City Park, behind Phipps Auditorium, featuring folk legend Ramblin' Jack Elliott, Jim Ringer, Mary McCaslin, Hot Rize, Rachel Faro, Kate Wolf and Norman and Nancy Blake. With the loss of the old concert hall, MASH booked its shows in a series of leased venues, including the Cherry Creek Gallery, the Events Center on Gaylord Street, West Auditorium, Phipps Auditorium, the Corkin Theatre at the Colorado Women's College at Montview and Quebec, First Unitarian Church Chapel on Lafayette, the back room of the Monastery and Conley's Nostalgia on South Broadway.

A folk original with a self-made cowboy image, Ramblin' Jack Elliott got his start in the 1950s bumming around with Woody Guthrie and influenced many in the following years, including Pete Seeger, Bob Dylan and Tom Russell.

Later in the year, MASH held a fundraising and organizational meeting to establish goals for the association in which they agreed that their primary organizational goals should be to "increase interest in the folk arts, promoting

The inimitable Bruce "Utah" Phillips championed folk music and labor unions throughout his life. He visited old pal Harry Tuft and friends at the new Denver Folklore Center before an evening performance at Swallow Hill Music Association. *Larry Schirkey.*

related programs, and increase the visibility of folk arts in the community." Additionally, MASH would act as a clearinghouse for folk arts information and pursue the establishment of a permanent facility to house folk arts programs, artifacts and organizations.

MASH held the First Denver Folk Festival on August 9, 1980, at the Colorado Women's College. The program extended from 11:00 a.m. until midnight and headlined nationally known artists Bruce "Utah" Phillips and Michael Cooney, ably supported by local artists, including the Mother Folkers, Grubstake, Roots & Branches, Rene Heredia, Sunday River Bluegrass Show, Dick Weissman, Dan & Chaz and Mary Flower. The show proved to be an artistic success but a financial disaster; the festival director quit just before the event took place, and MASH was left $2,000 in the red.

At the opposite end of the concert spectrum, MASH established a house concert series, which singer Jerry Rau kicked off on November 5, 1980. Embracing a long-standing folk tradition, artists performed in the intimate settings of people's homes, usually for fewer than twenty-five people. The series never made much money—the numbers were simply too small—but it presented a steady flow of fine musicians to a dedicated audience and enhanced the fledgling organization's name.

MASH survived because it had been founded on the Folklore Center's concert series and school. In spite of great energy from an enthusiastic band of volunteers, it was a rocky beginning, and it nearly went under more than once when a concert event cost more to produce than it brought in, leaving the cash flow strangled. Still, the folkies struggled forward. They established their first newsletter, *Simple Gifts*, in 1981, with Nancy Thorwardson manning the editor's chair. While some shows struggled to attract audiences, others made money. Hot Rize, the local bluegrass group made up of ex–Folklore Center employees (Charlie Sawtelle, Tim O'Brien, Nick Forster and Pete Wernick), was gaining a national reputation and packed listeners into three consecutive sold-out shows in 1981. It may have been a bit foolish, but undaunted by the previous year's loss, MASH presented the Second Annual Denver Folk Festival, this time at the Arvada Center, and at least did not lose

While best known as the founder and proprietor of the Denver Folklore Center, Harry Tuft (right) has always loved performing. Harry and his friends Steve Abbott (left) and Jack Stanesco (middle) have been together since 1972. *Swallow Hill Music Association.*

money. It also reached out to the community and established the Swallow Hill Troubadours, who provided free music to hospitals, nursing homes, schools and prisons.

By the beginning of 1983, MASH had nearly cleared up its debt. There was a small surge in membership, largely driven by people wanting to learn to play guitar, banjo and mandolin. But an unexpected blow came when, in March 1983, business conditions forced Rick Kirby to close the Folklore Center for good. Kirby fell prey to hard economic times, lagging interest in acoustic instruments and music and overall poor management, leaving Swallow Hill homeless, at least for a time.

Hey, School Girl

MASH initially moved its operations to the Capitol Hill Community Center at Williams Street and East Thirteenth Avenue. It continued to present concerts at a number of leased venues, but it was a struggle. Without a real permanent home, MASH was forced to suspend its school operations. The concerts were, at best, breaking even, but the organization had no steady cash flow on which it could count. With concerts, it was always hit or miss: a show might make a profit but just as easily could go in the red. There was little margin for error. Then MASH got a real shot of leadership and enthusiasm in 1984, when Julie Davis agreed to take over the school operation.

Nobody had deeper roots in the Denver folk community than Julie Davis, and she was an experienced music instructor who understood the instruction methods pioneered by the Chicago Old Town School of Folk Music and used at the Denver Folklore Center. Davis graduated in 1964 from East High School and wanted to continue in some way with music. She entered Adams State College, where she majored in history and music. She discovered she possessed a historian's passion for research, which she combined with her passion for music and explored the history of madrigals and other folk music forms. After graduation from Adams State, she moved to Charlottesville, Virginia, to pursue graduate studies in American history at the University of Virginia. Her stay in Charlottesville coincided with the sale of the Denver Folklore Center and the founding of MASH, during which time Davis maintained her connections to her Denver folk music friends and musicians, visiting with them whenever they came to play the Charlottesville area.

Julie Davis was one of the first people Harry Tuft hired to teach at the DFC. In the early 1980s, Julie played a pivotal role in establishing Swallow Hill Music Association's music school and keeping the organization afloat. *Swallow Hill Music Association.*

Julie returned to Denver in 1982 to take care of her ailing mother. She knew all the people involved in MASH, including Roz Brown, John Wolf from KVOD and Jeff Withers; they all had their roots in the Folklore Center community. But MASH's leadership was flagging; people were burned out, a situation not uncommon among volunteer-run nonprofits. They had put so much of their souls into MASH's survival, and the rewards were meager. Harry Tuft, who was working in real estate at the time and was not directly involved in Swallow Hill management, nevertheless approached Julie and asked if she might be willing to work with the organization, perhaps the school.

MASH certainly needed some fresh blood. The board had begun to think in terms of shutting down the entire operation, believing the whole folk movement had run its course and perhaps it was time to move on. Julie was not the least bit daunted at the prospect of restarting the school. When she previously worked at the Folklore Center, Phyllis Wagner had been the organizational force behind its school program. "And Phyllis was the most natural organizer I had been around. And I had been a good organizer as well. I had been president of my class, organized Girl Scouts, organized camps. But Phyllis was the best. It just came naturally. So when I came in to Swallow Hill, the organizing was natural to me." After some investigation, she created a business plan for the school and presented it to the board:

> I said, "Just give me six months. Let me make a presentation and give me six months. You don't have to pay me anything, just a commission on classes. Let me see if I can start the music school." It just felt like, well,

I had been living in small communities, and it felt like it was what was needed to me. It felt like it needed someone who believed it could work.

Over the years, Davis had noted that there were people willing to drive considerable distances for events—concerts and workshops—presented by the Folklore Center and MASH. She and her husband, Roy Laird, agreed to give it a try; he said he would support her with his carpentry work. Davis threw herself full time into organizing the school.

Organization skills or not, it wasn't going to be easy. MASH was located in leased space in the basement of the Capitol Hill Community Center, which, in Davis's words, "was just the pits; a tiny place. It didn't even have a teaching room. So we had to use these two teeny rooms. You couldn't even have the instrument cases in there. There was just enough room for a teacher, a pupil and a music stand. At night we would use the office."

But she was right. There was interest in the school. From the beginning, she organized workshops and some private lessons, and people came, especially to the workshops, which proved surprisingly popular. She recruited local folk singer Carla Sciaky to present a psaltery (a zither-like instrument) workshop, and to everyone's surprise, twenty-four people showed up. Who knew there were twenty-four people who even knew what a psaltery was? Eileen Niehouse, a wonderful finger-style guitarist, offered a DADGAD (an alternate tuning) guitar workshop, and thirty students attended. And nationally renowned musician John McCutcheon put on a successful hammered dulcimer workshop. "People were hungry to come back and hungry to learn more."

They used the big community room or the hall at the Capitol Hill Community Center for the workshops and continued using the dinky, dank basement space for private lessons. Teachers included Ron Jones (guitar, fiddle), Richard Reed (blues and finger-style guitar), Carla Sciaky (guitar, voice), Eileen Niehouse (DADGAD and Celtic guitar) and Doug Birch (dulcimer). As demand increased, they added banjo, mandolin, bass and harmonica instruction.

The school's success reenergized MASH members and the community. Eileen Niehouse joined the board; soon, others pitched in, bringing more fresh blood, ideas and, most of all, energy. New members came from the old Folklore Center community, as well as the folk dance community, which had always had a strong and faithful following.

With five hundred members in 1985, and Julie Davis the acting director of nearly everything, Swallow Hill knew it needed to find more permanent quarters. One day, board member Richard Reed was driving in South Denver when he spotted a For Rent sign on a converted house at 1905 South Pearl Street. He immediately went to the Community Center and brought Davis and Niehouse to investigate. They thought: it just might work.

5

SWALLOW HILL—A NEW HOME

The new facility was rustic—and decidedly cozy; small might be a better term—but it was the best Swallow Hill could afford at the time and certainly an improvement over the Community Center. Skyloom Fibers had originally transformed the building into a storefront, and Leo Instruments now occupied the space. Bruce Leo Anderson, the former proprietor of the Zither Shop, built dulcimers and instrument kits. (Dulcimers are three- or four-stringed Appalachian instruments. The player holds the instrument on his lap and strums the strings with a pick in the right hand while fretting the strings with the left-hand fingers or with a small wooden dowel.) Anderson agreed to pay one-third of the rent. It seemed like a good fit for Swallow Hill. It agreed to a three-year lease.

Swallow Hill moved in immediately and held concerts and classes in the same space. Davis took charge of the space during the day, presenting a combination of private and group classes for a variety of instruments and styles. Concert director Janet Wong initiated a concert series, New Faces in Denver Folk, which presented a number of local musicians, including Willie and Carol, Spencer Bohren, Bonnie Carol and Linda Maitch, who all went on to national recognition.

At night, they cleared out the space, set up rented chairs (they had no space to store them) and presented their shows. Julie recalled:

> *It was an intimate concert space, but so many people loved it, and the players really loved it. It was when Swallow Hill was put on the map because the performers loved working there, so close to the audience. There was a community connected to it. It was, for the performers, different from*

just going in to a place to play. It was more like visiting family. We were inundated with calls to book acts."

The relationship worked two ways. The audience came to trust those booking the concerts. Reminiscent of the 1960s, many concertgoers came to shows without knowing the artists. Swallow Hill gained a trusted reputation for bringing in solid, interesting artists, and people came out for the shows.

"I was working on the school, and it was growing," recalls Davis.

I feel one of my contributions to Swallow Hill is the culture. I wanted people who were well known in the community to teach—Mary Flower [blues singer], Mary Stribling [bass player extraordinaire]—people who were out [performing], and people could say, "I could take lessons from that person at Swallow Hill." But I did not want people who were self-absorbed. I wanted it to be about the student. I was on a search for people who could play. But many who can are not good teachers. I think it says something that a big number of people I brought in here are still teaching here or elsewhere in Denver.

While Julie worked full time at the school, her husband, Roy Laird, donated his time and skills. Laird, Bruce Anderson of Leo Instruments and Bruce Burnell built a new staircase, constructed and soundproofed the lesson rooms and erected the stage. Laird went on to become one of the Tattered Cover Book Store's general managers.

Growth was solid, especially in the school, but the stress was taking its toll. Davis and concert director Wong were paid on commission: if a show or class went well, they made money; if it tanked, they didn't. There were other organizational issues. "So, after all this, I was getting completely burned out. The board had a vision of what it should be. And I came to the conclusion that we couldn't move on until the concert and school directors were paid at least a partial salary. I came to realize that I couldn't advocate for that and be the recipient of it." At the time, the school was making money, and concerts were, at best, breaking even.

AMAZING GRACE

Julie Davis announced that she was resigning as school director, feeling that she had done all that she could to establish a stable music education

organization. Swallow Hill advertised for a new school director. The ad
read: "Wanted: director of folk music school. Low pay."

Seth Weisberg responded. Weisberg was born in 1961 in Huntington,
West Virginia, the third of five children. His father owned the successful
State Electric Supply Company in this industrial city of some seventy-
five thousand on the shores of the Ohio River. As a youngster, Weisberg
showed some interest in music, took piano and played in a local rock
group. As devout Jews, his parents regularly attended synagogue, where
Seth heard Jewish sacred music. While attending Jewish summer camp,
he encountered Israeli folk music, which was popular at the time. One
summer, he attended the West Virginia Folk Festival, where he saw, for the
first time, people playing dulcimers and singing Appalachian folk music.
It planted a bug in his brain.

Inspiration—or obsession, some might say—comes on people in strange
ways. After high school, Seth set out for Washington University in St. Louis,
looking to get away from small-city West Virginia and stretch his horizons a
bit. He wrangled a non-paying job hosting a jazz program on the university's
radio station. But at the same time, the magic of folk music pulled him back.
At a time when commercial folk music was dead, he discovered Harry Smith's
seminal collection, *The Anthology of American Folk Music*. Originally released in
1952, Smith's eighty-four-song collection covered the gamut of American folk
sounds, including such diversity as Appalachian ballads (Clarence Ashely's
"The House Carpenter"), mountain string bands (Carolina Tar Heels' "Peg
and Awl"), blues (Mississippi John Hurt's "Frankie"), popular folk music
(the Carter Family's "Engine 143") and sacred music (the Alabama Sacred
Harp Singers' "Rocky Road"). Like Bob Dylan and others before him, the
young Weisberg was captivated. By his own admission, instead of studying,
he listened to every ethnic recording in the university library, from drums
to ballads to African chants. And much to the dismay of his audience, he
began introducing folk recordings on his jazz show. That "non-conformity"
got him fired from the job.

After switching from engineering to economics, he graduated, unsure of
what he wanted to do, but he was sure that he did not want to go back to West
Virginia and work in the family business, at least not at that time. Having
married a Colorado girl he met during his senior year on a visit to Boulder, he
decided to move to Denver, where, if nothing else, his in-laws might provide
free babysitting for the couple's new baby. He was just twenty-two.

They moved into a small Washington Park rental house owned by his
in-laws, and Seth applied for teaching jobs. He taught economics at the

Seth Weisberg, here in front of Swallow Hill's Pearl Street location, kept the organization going through some of its toughest times in the mid-'80s and into the '90s.

Community College of Denver but jumped when he saw the ad for Swallow Hill. He arrived at Swallow Hill for an interview with Eileen Niehouse and Julie Davis. He recalls, "I was working my damnedest to impress them, and little did I know they were working their damnedest to reel me in." Both Davis and Niehouse were burned out on the long hours and low pay and were ready to move on to other projects. "I realized that they didn't have anyone else. The last guy bowed out because it was a hell of a lot of work, and he couldn't make any money at it. Too many pieces to keep going; too hard to keep the board pleased," Seth remembered.

They hired Seth immediately. Eileen Niehouse left within a week.

He was ambitious, a real go-getter. They proposed to pay him $200 a week plus a cut of the fees for lessons he booked. "I was pretty successful. If you got on the phone with me, you were probably going to come in. And if you came in, you would probably book a lesson. And if you came for lessons, you would probably take a membership." He proved to be a remarkably good salesman.

There were organizational troubles, the kind most nonprofit volunteer organizations go through. "The organization had gotten to the point where there wasn't a clear nucleus of people invested in keeping [it] alive." Some early board members had come back in 1985, when Julie Davis had reconstituted the school and given Swallow Hill new focus. The organization had put some of the active volunteers on the board, but people were not much interested in donating cash, and there was confusion over who was serving and who was being served.

While Harry Tuft was not involved in Swallow Hill's day-to-day operations, he cast a long shadow over it and Denver's folk music community. He taught a few guitar classes each week but was not engaged at the time in any of Swallow Hill's business or organizational decisions. Yet his influence had significant impact on Swallow Hill, though not always to the organization's benefit. Seth, as a Denver newcomer, had not yet become fully aware of the Tuft legacy:

> *In 1986 or so, we had a benefit concert, and the proceeds went into someone's bank account. And, in 1987, they decided to disperse the funds. They decided to give Tuft $3,000 to help organize his record collection at his house and someone to help him with the computer to get it all listed. And I was pretty outraged. I was pretty bold at the time. "Dammit, this [Swallow Hill] is where it is happening. We're the folk people. We're doing it all. He's not doing it!" Now, I was too young in the organization to say that.*

In the end, though, Seth was able to convince the board that it was unwise to spend the funds in such a way. It was a rough way to start out, but regardless of the decision, Tuft and Weisberg became close friends and confidants over time.

In 1986, Swallow Hill had 550 paying members, but cash flow remained a problem. Weisberg set about implementing changes both within the school and in the organization as a whole, but he was young and working against a typical newcomer's problem. "I knew how to drive a business, but I didn't know all the people. I didn't know who Harry was." Seth contends that Judith Joyner, then concert director, knew Celtic music, so she booked a lot of it, but she did not know agents or contracts. And there was confusion about who and what Swallow Hill was and what business strategies were appropriate. Both board members and volunteers thought they had tried everything to raise awareness and money. Seth contends that part of the confusion was in defining the term "folk music." "There was an idea that we did not book bluegrass music." Many thought that it was not folk music or that bluegrass musicians had their own organization that would promote it. To make matters worse, he added, "Hell, we didn't know what a marketing campaign was. But we knew the Music Association of Swallow Hill didn't sound as good as the Swallow Hill Music Association."

Apparently, early board members had been enamored with the TV sitcom *M*A*S*H* and wanted to have that acronym, but it wasn't a marketing success. The general public remained unclear about what Swallow Hill was. Over time, the organization changed its name to Swallow Hill Music Association, placing more emphasis on "Swallow Hill" and less on "music." "And we had a flowery logo," Weisberg recalled, adding, "Then we got rid of the flowery logo and went to more of a woodcut look that was more rustic, more Americana. Then Judith Joyner came up with 'Your Home for Acoustic Music' because people wanted acoustic in there." To highlight the change, Leo Anderson designed the woodcut logo and made the first sign. Step by small step, Swallow Hill expanded its folk music vision and definition to a more inclusive purview that embraced bluegrass, ragtime, drumming and all manner of ethnic music. There was some initial resistance, Seth recollected:

> But people realized that we weren't putting drumming in the middle of their bluegrass concert, so the conflict wasn't serious. It was really about making money to keep the place going; having more programs, more ways to bring you in, a broader target. The definition had to be broader for a community-

based organization. It had to be more than just white guitar players doing the specific ballad-driven tradition. There was a flowering over time of what became "world music." There was, for example, a greater array of Cajun music, African music, Tejano music, and people were more conscious of presenting it.

Swallow Hill also embraced dance, not just American folk or square dancing, but other ethnic representations, including Cajun and zydeco.

By 1988, Swallow Hill boasted a membership of eight hundred and a mailing list of four thousand. The 1980s had been a generally bleak time for folk and acoustic music, but the worst times seemed to be in the past. In spite of the rise of MTV (or maybe because of it and other cable TV–based entertainment, like CMT), guitar sales began to recover and interest in acoustic music regained a foothold in the cultural landscape. Paul Simon released his landmark album *Graceland* in 1986, the same year British singer/songwriter Peter Gabriel released *So*. Simon worked in the folk-rock-pop vein, while Gabriel continued to develop his art-rock approach, and both artists integrated African rhythms and instruments into the mix, giving listeners a texture not previously heard. Other artists followed suit, adding Celtic, Cajun and other ethnic sounds to their musical palettes and shining more light on ethnic music sources. Gabriel and Simon embraced MTV and music video, putting a greater visual emphasis on their work. As the 1980s came to a close, folk and acoustic music did not regain the prominence it had held in the early 1960s, but it was no longer entertainment's bastard stepchild.

HOMEWARD BOUND

When Leo Instruments vacated its Pearl Street space in 1989, Swallow Hill moved to take over the entire building, all 2,500 square feet. That fall, Seth became executive director and launched Swallow Hill's first-ever successful capital campaign, which allowed for the purchase of the Pearl Street facility for $97,000. Owning its own facility proved to be a significant milestone for the still struggling organization.

But even as it broadened its musical definition, most observers still pictured Swallow Hill as a white man's organization that did not—or could not—represent the cultural traditions of Denver's people of color. This was in stark contrast to the image of the folk tradition. The folk music community that grew out of the 1950s and '60s prided itself on inclusion; they were the first to openly embrace black blues and Celtic and Israeli music, along with the long-standing English-Scottish ballad tradition. But by the 1980s, the African American community had turned its back on the blues; older blacks saw it as music tied to the South, the plantations and oppression, while younger blacks were embracing the sounds of the city represented by dance music and rhythm and blues, which morphed, over time, into hip-hop and rap. In an odd turn, it was a white audience that bought blues recordings and attended concerts. Still, Swallow Hill wanted to reach out to Denver's ethnic communities. This was not easy. Seth remembered one telling conversation:

> *Tony Garcia, of Su Teatro* [Denver's leading Hispanic theater and music group], *was saying, "Seth, you and your white Anglo-Saxon traditions are not going to be appropriate for our traditions," and I said, "Tony, look at me; I'm a Jewish guy from Poland, okay? I don't know what you're talking about. And if you want to get on the board, get on the board." But his* [Tony's] *identity was that they had to have their own place and their own things. It was part of the ongoing political struggle in this country. You know, "Let me into the mainstream, you're ghettoizing me!" Then, "What? I'm in the mainstream now? You're watering me down! I'm gonna lose my ghetto where I have my cultural sense."*

Even as it expanded its definition and offerings, Swallow Hill could not, much to Seth's chagrin, completely shed its "white loaf" reputation.

WHAT DID YOU LEARN IN SCHOOL TODAY?

Under Weisberg's leadership, the early 1990s saw Swallow Hill refurbish its Pearl Street building. Growth was steady, and the facility was soon bursting at the seams, with no space for classroom expansion, the most critical need. The building featured a small concert space that seated about one hundred people, just right for intimate performances. When an artist could draw a larger crowd, Swallow Hill would lease larger halls, like nearby Cameron Church on South Pearl Street. As they expanded their operations and public profile, Seth sought and won, for the first time, significant grants from the

Scientific and Cultural Facilities Tax District (SCFD) and from the Colorado Council for the Arts and Humanities. The additional funds allowed for extended hours of operation and provided concert series support. In 1990, Rebecca "Becky" Miklitch joined the staff as assistant school director and made a significant impact.

Becky was born in Honolulu, where her father taught psychology at the University of Hawaii. She grew up in Lakewood with her brother, who was a gifted and serious student dedicated to the sciences. Rather than compete with her brother, Becky decided to distinguish herself in other ways. She liked music and enrolled in recorder and flute lessons. Her father gave her brother a guitar in an effort to expand his interests beyond science. When the guitar languished for months in her brother's room, she adopted it. She had already spent hours sitting with her mother's records and had memorized every John Denver song she found. Right away, she took to the guitar and after high school spent a year studying music in Norway before entering Colgate University in 1986 as a language major. There she found she could sing and play at a local coffeehouse and get paid for it. And she enjoyed it. After bouncing from one major to another, she graduated Phi Beta Kappa in 1990 with a major in music and a minor in psychology.

She returned to Denver with little or no direction in mind but was determined not to be a part of what she termed "the evil establishment." After a week or more looking for jobs, Becky spied an ad in a Swallow Hill brochure looking for someone to assist at the school. In spite of growing up in Lakewood, she knew little about Denver's cultural underground and nothing about Swallow Hill, but the job sounded intriguing. She noticed that applications were due at 4:00 p.m. that afternoon, and it was already 3:45 p.m., but she called to inquire. As luck would have it, she talked to Seth, who in his laid-back manner told her not to worry and that she should come down and chat with him. Throwing on what she called "sensible clothes" (meaning something other than the cutoff jeans she had on), she arrived at Swallow Hill's South Pearl Street facility within the hour; Seth met her and whisked her into one of the practice rooms for an interview. She learned that someone else had been hired for the position and fired within the last few weeks, and the job was open again. But she balked: was she willing to work evenings and weekends, twenty hours a week, for a paltry five dollars an hour? What would her friends think? Or, for that matter, her parents? But Seth was insistent—and charming—and with a little arm-twisting, he had a new part-time employee. Her title was assistant school director, but "basically I was hired to answer the phone," she recollected, "because the business had gotten to the point that that it was too much for Seth to handle by himself. So, my job was to be the front office."

She jumped into what she called "the lovable chaos" that was Swallow Hill. On her first day, Seth was trying to repair an inexpensive table, and since Swallow Hill was always broke, he had a few two-by-fours in his hand and asked Miklitch, the music major, to help him. "So there I was. I was whining about it, trying to use a saw, and Seth turns to me and says, 'Ah, in the long tradition of Swallow Hill, women strong of mind and weak of arm,'" she laughed. "That was day one at work." Though the pay wasn't great, it at least allowed her to move into a basement apartment.

Almost immediately, her hours changed when Seth asked her to come in on Saturday mornings and help manage the new guitar classes Harry Tuft was teaching. As another Swallow Hill newcomer, she had no idea who Harry was or what role he had played in Denver folk music, but she agreed:

Now, if you know anything about Harry and the hours he keeps, and me, the incredible night owl I am, having Harry and me together on Saturday mornings at nine o'clock was a really, really bad idea. Harry and I got off to such a bad start. We were both so not morning people. Plus, Harry and I are always running late. It was like both of us were going against each other's nature. We'd both get there, we'd both be late and we'd both be mad that the other was late and hadn't gotten there early enough to get the chairs set up. Harry was always mad that I wasn't there ten minutes before him to make the coffee. And I, of course, was pissed off that some man thought I was there to make coffee for him! I mean, I don't drink this stuff. If you want coffee, you can damn well make it yourself! I'm a liberated woman, and I don't make coffee for no man!

She laughed. They got off on the wrong foot but soon became good friends and learned to work together.

"I don't remember *ever* working twenty hours a week. One thing's for sure, I had no social life." The school was fairly well organized at the time, and then shortly after Becky came on board, the school switched the teaching staff from being on straight commission to salary, a strategy necessary for survival. But it was never just a job. She was working thirty-plus hours a week, getting paid for twenty and learning that it was a community and an organization that operated on the goodwill and help of many people. It was a real adjustment, but one that she made willingly. "It never is just a job here. I see it when I hire teachers. You know within a month if they are going to make the adjustment. It is all about community. If they don't get it, they'll think that Swallow Hill is just abusing them. And if they do, they'll just love it and want to do whatever they can for it."

About 1991, she recalled:

> I don't remember if I was full time or not, because everything was in this constant state of Jell-O, but I remember unloading packets of the new newsletter. It's always exciting when the newsletter comes in and you leaf through it and see what it's like. So I opened it up, and I'm paging through and I get to the staff page, and I see: "Rebecca Miklitch, School Director." And I went, "Huh?" And Seth says, "Oh, yeah, I thought I'd make you school director. I thought it'd make you feel good to get that official title."

Unbeknownst to Becky, Swallow Hill had received a grant, which funded an executive director position, and Seth, who had young children at the time, was trying to get off an evening schedule. Though he meant it in a sweet way, it meant greater responsibility and not much more authority for her. And no pay increase initially. "It was laughable, in those days. I got on full time and got a raise to seven dollars an hour, but there was no health insurance. My parents were asking, 'Why are you doing this?' My father thought it was just a phase. 'She'll grow out of it.' Meanwhile, my brother was getting his PhD; he's a noted physicist, and he's publishing papers, and I'm the black sheep of the family," she said with a smile and a wink.

While the concert series was the public face of Swallow Hill, with many non-members attending shows presented at numerous Denver locations, the school was the moneymaker. When Seth joined the Swallow Hill staff, the school stuck mostly to the tried-and-true guitar, banjo, mandolin and bass classes. But Seth sought to expand the school's offerings to include instruction in drumming, harmonica and Dobro, as well as playing styles thought by some to be outside the folk milieu. Where else might you find a class on how to fingerpick Beatles tunes? Or play Irish flute? They all fit in with the ever-changing definition of folk music as "acoustic music in many styles." But Becky wanted to expand it further still and, to Weisberg's dismay, got rid of some of the "old-fashioned" offerings. She wanted to drop the Carter Family guitar lessons, arguing that there were too few takers. Seth resisted. Becky won.

RECOGNITION

By the mid-1990s, Swallow Hill seemed to be on footing that appeared more solid than in the past, even though it constantly struggled for funds. In a letter to the Colorado Council on Humanities and the Arts endorsing Swallow Hill's nomination for a Governor's Award, Marc Shulgold, music critic for the *Rocky Mountain News*, wrote:

> *Swallow Hill fills a large void in the Denver area—and fills it well. The mix of "star" attractions and more obscure, but equally deserving ones, is generally well managed. Also commendable is the Association's support of Hispanic and other ethnic styles...Performers always speak praise as part of their onstage patter.*

In 1995, there were some 2,000 paying members and a mailing list of 25,000, while the school employed 35 teachers who instructed more than 750 students annually. With the addition of concert director Meredith Carson, the concert offerings rose to a new level as Swallow Hill attracted an increasing number of nationally known acts, as well as deserving but less well-known local performers.

Needing to recharge her batteries, Becky took the summer off in 1992, an unpaid leave of absence. She was having boyfriend problems, and the stress at Swallow Hill and the low pay did nothing to help. She spent the summer working at a camp as its music education director. She had worked there previously and had been invited back. It was a good break.

After years of struggling for the smallest attention, the real growth began. Swallow Hill had its newly refurbished facility on South Pearl Street and for the first time had enough room. There had always been a demand for new and additional classes, but there was no way to pay the staff more money without an increase in business. There was additional incentive: Deidre Shaffer, one of the board members, was determined that the staff should finally get benefits. At budget time, each department devised a plan on how it would increase revenue that would net the required annual income to pay for benefits. As it worked out, Carson's expanded concert plan failed to meet expectations, but Miklitch's expanded school plan netted twice its projected revenue. And the staff got health insurance and other benefits for the first time.

There was friction between these two competitive and talented women, something that increased over time as the school made more money, attracting an ever-increasing number of students to a widening array of classes, and the concert series netted less and less as the operating costs increased. Internally, it boiled down to competition for scarce resources, and Swallow Hill was always broke. On more than one occasion, the organization's future was on the line based on the success or failure of a big show. Bankruptcy was never far away.

Becky claims that most teachers live below the poverty line. Teachers are a special breed of musicians who eke out a meager living through a combination of teaching and playing whatever live gigs are available, from private parties to shows to clubs. On paper, it would appear that teachers make a good hourly wage, but that is misleading. An instructor might be at the school for six to eight hours but would get paid only for the couple of hours he or she actually taught. It is definitely a source of stress within the Swallow Hill community.

It isn't just the teachers. The prevailing myth holds that performers are, if not overpaid, at least nicely compensated. Star performers fill halls and collect fees in the tens, if not hundreds, of thousands of dollars, but most performers work on commission, usually tied to a portion of the gate receipts *after* the house deducts expenses. Becky recalled a story that serves as a good example. At the first weekend concert she worked at Swallow Hill, she had the responsibility of setting up the room, managing volunteers and collecting proceeds. That Saturday evening, Swallow Hill presented the Country Gentlemen, one of America's foremost and best-loved bluegrass bands, a group with a national reputation and numerous recordings in its portfolio. After counting up the till and subtracting the promotion fees, she could not quite believe what the numbers told her. Here were four outstanding musicians who had just played their hearts out in a fine show to a sold-out room. They netted $288 for their efforts. "A Saturday night. The 'big money night.' And they're on the road! They have to pay for gas and hotels!"

As time passed, Becky took complete charge of the school, while Seth took on more of the day-to-day responsibilities of the management beyond the school. It was not a power play on Seth's part; it was a practical development. Seth believed it freed others up to put their energies into focusing on more immediate needs. It seemed to work.

6

A Changing of the Guard

In 1995, after eight successful years at Swallow Hill, Seth Weisberg approached the board of directors and told it that he was resigning from the position of executive director; he agreed to stay on through the search for his replacement. He felt as if he had given all that he could and had taken Swallow Hill as far as he was capable. He intended to return to his family's business. During his time at Swallow Hill, he had survived on slim paychecks, in no small part because of his devoted in-laws, who had rented him a house and often bought new clothing for his children. Food had not been much of a problem because he was part of a food co-op and kept a garden. Still, while he had served as executive director, he and his family had taken no vacations and never went out to dinner. And they had no TV or stereo.

"When I left Swallow Hill, I didn't leave because of the money; but the moment the other paychecks came in, I realized how poor we really were. We bought a bed, a new bed. We bought a stereo. We filled the pantry with food. We bought our son a new baseball glove. We had just worn down the whole capital base of the Weisberg household. We just didn't buy things for a long time."

Swallow Hill had come a long way under Weisberg's enthusiastic leadership. The school's teachers instructed more than 1,500 students annually; Swallow Hill had qualified for a $7,500 Denver Foundation grant; *Westword*, Denver's alternative weekly newspaper, had named Swallow Hill Denver's "Best Folk Music Venue"; and the concert series presented more than one hundred shows in 1995, featuring such notable artists as Tim

O'Brien and Jerry Douglas, Celeste Krenz, Carla Sciaky, Tom Paxton, BeauSoleil, Grubstake, Battlefield Band, Triple Play (Kevin Welch, Jimmy LaFave and Michael Fracasso), Jean Redpath, Tish Hinojosa, Garnet Rodgers, Clive Gregson, John Renbourn and Robin Williamson, Katy Moffatt and Dan Crary.

The board of directors immediately set about finding Weisberg's replacement. More than fifty candidates, many of them apparently qualified, applied. Some board members approached Becky Miklitch and inquired about her availability. She was flattered. "But you know, Meredith Carson is a very head-strong person. She's, what, fifteen years older than me? And there were issues between us, mostly about funding and resources. There was no way I could be Meredith's boss and would never have the board's backing in it. So I didn't apply for the position."

The board narrowed it down to six or seven candidates. All but one of them turned it down when they heard the salary: $24,000 a year.

ROCK-AND-ROLL MAN

After months of searching, the board appeared ready to name a replacement when local bandleader and musician Chris Daniels applied. Even though Daniels was educated and interested, some board members, including Harry Tuft and Seth Weisberg, were initially lukewarm. Daniels was not what might be termed "your typical folky."

Chris Daniels bristles with energy and enthusiasm even when he is not on stage. Medium height and wiry, with close-cropped, light-colored hair and intense blue eyes, he seems to be in constant motion. Chris was born in 1952 in St. Paul, Minnesota; his father was an executive in the agriculture business and his mother a homemaker. By his own admission, he was an indifferent and somewhat rebellious student, something that may have had to do with what he terms his "raging dyslexia." After his expulsion from a private school in Minnesota, his parents enrolled him in Colorado Academy. Chris took up the guitar at the age of ten but did not study it, or music, formally with teachers. Yet he had become an adept musician by the time he was eighteen. When he dropped out of college, he said his parents disowned him, so he moved to Colorado in 1970, spending his time jamming with an array of local musicians. He lived in a commune in Eldorado Springs, sleeping in a converted school bus. In 1971, he joined the Colorado musical group Magic Music, writing songs for it during a period when it briefly flirted with a national recording contract. It was at this time that Daniels played his first gig for Harry Tuft at the Denver Folklore Center. He finally came to the realization that he needed formal musical training and education, and he entered McAllister College in Minneapolis, getting his BA in journalism. He also studied music theory at Berklee College of Music in Boston, completing four years of study in three years between 1976 and 1979.

After graduation, Daniels played in the band Spoons with his friend, Sam Broussard, a Louisiana-born guitarist who had backed Michael Martin Murphy. He then spent two years touring with Russell Smith, the former leader of the Amazing Rhythm Aces, who had a national hit in 1976 with "Third Rate Romance" and won a Grammy the following year for "The End Is Not in Sight." It was a valuable learning experience for the young Daniels, and when Smith decided to move to Nashville and get off the road, Daniels elected to form his own band—Chris Daniels and the Kings, a group that combined the sounds of rock-and-roll and rhythm and blues with horns, similar to the Average White Band or Tower of Power. The band proved to be an immediate hit with the college crowd, many of whom had never experienced a live, dance-oriented band with a full array of horns. Ultimately, Chris Daniels and the Kings proved to be more popular in Europe than in America and played an extensive tour there each year, selling a considerable number of albums and CDs on each trip. Sandwiched between tours of the United States and Europe, Daniels returned to college and secured an MA in history from the University of Colorado, Boulder. By 1995, radio had changed its play format yet again and squeezed out bands like the Kings, and with band revenues slumping, Chris applied for the executive director's job at Swallow Hill Music Association.

At first, neither Harry Tuft, the "godfather of Denver folk music" and influential Swallow Hill board member, nor Seth Weisberg was impressed with Daniels. Harry seemed more swayed by Chris's image as a hard-rocking singer/guitarist than his education or credentials as a businessman who had successfully led and managed a band and balanced its books, but Seth soon took to Daniels, believing that he might bring unique management skills and especially a high energy level to the position. Chris was eventually able to overcome most, but not all, of the resistance on the board—some of whom never saw how a rock-and-roller could lead a folk music school—and secured the position of executive director. He was to start September 1, 1995; the pay was $24,000 per year.

Seth recommended that Chris spend the month of August shadowing him, a month of unpaid on-the-job training. Chris agreed, believing it would

When Chris Daniels became Swallow Hill's executive director in 1995, his reputation as a rocker left some people with doubt about his commitment to folk music. They were wrong. *Swallow Hill Music Association.*

be the best way to become familiar with his responsibilities and the staff personnel. His first official day on the job, September 1, started with a bang. Becky Miklitch, the dynamic school director, who had done an outstanding job expanding the school's offerings and enrollment, dropped by his office and stated that if she were to continue, she needed a raise. Later the same day, Meredith Carson, Swallow Hill's successful concert director, visited Daniels and said that if she were to continue, she, too, needed a raise. The following day, Daniels learned that, for all practical purposes, Swallow Hill was flat out of operating funds and would soon be broke if it could not find additional income.

The situation might have cowed a weaker person, but not Chris. Through his internship with Seth, he understood the cyclical nature of Swallow Hill's revenue stream, which stemmed primarily from membership (the steadiest and most predictable income), newsletter advertising, concerts (something of a loss-leader) and the school (the most consistently profitable operation). Additional funding came from SCFD grants, but just that year, the SCFD had voted to reduce funding from $20,000 per year to $10,000. One SCFD board member, a black woman, perceived a lack of diversity in Swallow Hill membership and program participation, something that was at the time perhaps true, but it stung the leadership to be perceived as biased. Folk music has a long and storied history of involvement with civil rights and has always embraced black and minority music as essential parts of its makeup. But minority participation in Swallow Hill programs and events was, indeed, low; folk music simply had little appeal to the majority of Denver's minority populations. Even B.B. King, the great black blues singer, has noted that, since the late 1960s, his audience and that of other blues singers have been almost entirely white. Still, Swallow Hill had not been active in reaching out to the broader community, and the SCFD funding cut stood.

In the short run, there was little Chris could do about changing SCFD funding, but he immediately set out to raise additional funds from sources he knew in the community. He successfully found donors who provided an additional $20,000 in funding, and Swallow Hill ended fiscal 1995 some $2,000 in the black, a small but important lesson in fundraising and a credit to Daniels's management talents and leadership. As it entered 1996, the overriding issues Swallow Hill faced were fundraising, space, public relations and operations, all tied in some way to one another.

As for operations, the school had been, for some time, a significant source of operating revenue. Rebecca Miklitch, the school's director, continued to successfully grow the school year after year. Whenever—and wherever—more space became available, she put it to use creating new classes and, most importantly, filling them. The Pearl Street facility was bursting at the seams, with every available space used for classes and administration. Swallow Hill continued to present shows in the one-hundred-seat performance space at Pearl Street and leased space when needed, which, with one hundred shows a year, was more often than not. On the balance, concerts, at best, added little to the bottom line. Becky argued that Swallow Hill should seek additional classroom space, and since classes were the moneymakers, the school should take over the concert space, and Swallow Hill should consider curtailing the concert schedule.

It comes as no surprise that Meredith Carson, the concert director, disagreed. She argued that, while it was true that the concerts did not add considerably to the bottom line, they were the main source of publicity. Many concertgoers were not members, and after attending a Swallow Hill concert, some became aware of the association for the first time and often joined. Concerts provided much-needed publicity in the papers and folk music publications, and it was, in Meredith's view, the concerts that provided Swallow Hill with much of its public face. She also had a vision for Swallow Hill's music program: in her mind, Swallow Hill's concerts represented something special in the community, where such music—contemporary and traditional folk and acoustic music—had few other outlets. No radio stations, let alone television, programmed this type of music, and Swallow Hill represented its only outlet. Concert attendance provided sufficient proof of the music's popularity; in 1996, there were more than 110 shows, with an average attendance of two hundred people per show.

Chris understood the wisdom of both arguments, and his solution took two routes. First, he sought to revise Swallow Hill's mission statement so that there would be no confusion about the organization's stated goals: its two main focuses would be education *and* concerts. The board quickly agreed. The second part of the solution was to lease additional space, which he quickly found in the buildings across Pearl Street and around the corner on Jewell Avenue. After signing a lease, Chris moved nearly all the administrative offices to the new space, freeing up space in the main building for additional classrooms. Becky was not one to hesitate; within six months, she had filled all the classrooms with a steady stream of new offerings. She clamored for more space. At the same time, Chris encouraged Meredith to continue to expand her concert offerings while utilizing leased space for shows.

Chris had to face the main issue before him: the 1905 South Pearl Street building was simply inadequate to meet Swallow Hill's growing needs. The

Singer/songwriter Dave Alvin emerged in the late 1980s to help establish Americana as a "new" musical genre. Alvin says, "There are two types of folk music: quiet folk music and loud folk music. I play both." Does he ever. *Swallow Hill Music Association.*

A gifted guitarist, singer and writer, Cliff Eberhardt is a compelling performer. His songs show that his influences include the likes of Joni Mitchell and James Taylor, as well as Muddy Waters and Howlin' Wolf. Eclectic. *Swallow Hill Music Association.*

matter was not new. Seth Weisberg had begun to consider alternatives before he stepped down. Knowing that space was a never-ending issue, Seth had initially proposed that Swallow Hill buy the building lot next door, but it was unable to secure the $7,000 purchase price. Sometime later, he suggested a major overhaul to the building. With about 2,500 square feet available, it was clearly inadequate, and Seth contacted an architectural firm, which designed an addition that, if built, would raise the usable space to about 6,500 square feet. The addition would cost $500,000.

This, of course, raised a central issue: Swallow Hill had no track record when it came to fundraising. No one on the staff or among the volunteers had any experience in it, and the board of directors took no leadership on the issue. Nevertheless, the board authorized a capital campaign with the expressed goal of raising the half-million dollars needed for the Pearl Street expansion, but by the time Chris took over, it had made little progress toward the goal, and the campaign seemed to have stalled out even before it was underway. To make matters more complex, Chris began to doubt the wisdom of expanding the existing facility. By the end of 1996, it was apparent to him that 6,500 square feet would be inadequate to meet current needs, let alone provide for the future. Seth had not wanted or could not face the eventuality of finding another facility; he had put his heart and soul into Pearl Street and saw it as the only real home Swallow Hill had known.

Daniels's view was more analytical and less emotional. While the Pearl Street building was warm and cozy and had seen its share of historic concerts, it could never grow to meet the needs of an organization that was experiencing substantial growth. In his mind, the board faced a clear but tough decision: either find land for expansion or begin looking to relocate. The building expansion would never fly, but the board remained, at least for the moment, committed to the expansion project.

So Chris quietly began the search for a possible new home. He learned that Sandy Gurtler and those who represented the original Elitch Gardens were looking for someone to take over the old and famous Elitch's Theatre. Chris, Meredith and Becky went to investigate and were impressed by the size of the old theater, which could easily hold one thousand concertgoers, had a good stage and boasted more than acceptable acoustics. Other buildings on the site could be converted to classrooms and administrative offices, and Gurtler was willing to donate the building free of charge to Swallow Hill. But further investigation showed that the Elitch's site would require substantially more than $500,000 in needed repairs and modifications, probably closer to $1 million, and the property was outside the area that Swallow Hill considered its neighborhood.

Before he could brief the board, word of Daniels's visit to Elitch's leaked out to the press, and board members learned about it through the newspapers. They were not happy to hear about the supposed relocation, which they had not yet approved, but Chris faced them at the next meeting and was able to convince them that the papers had misquoted him and Gurtler and that he had made no deal.

The assessment process continued. Chris investigated a number of warehouses located near Interstate 25 and Speer Boulevard, but they, too, proved unsuitable. Then he located the then vacant South Broadway Christian Church at First and Lincoln Avenues and convinced Harry to go with him to investigate. The church facility was nearly perfect: a large performance space where the main meeting hall had been and an attached school that would provide plenty of classroom space and administrative offices. Chris thought it was perfect, but when they returned to the car and began to discuss it, Harry was less than enthusiastic. There was, he pointed out, no parking lot and limited on-street parking, not to mention the intrusive noise from the traffic at that busy intersection. Chris stubbornly disagreed. He said, "You don't understand what I'm saying. It's perfect." Harry responded, "I *do* understand what you are saying; I just disagree with you."

Chris's background as a performer gave him a certain perspective on space that placed a great emphasis on the performance aspects. After all, as a bandleader, he knew performance and flash mattered. The conflict with some staff and board members came in this area of image. Becky believed that Chris thought that a LoDo site would be better for performances and would expand the concert audience, allowing Swallow Hill to make concerts more profitable. Becky, on the other hand, wanted to maintain the profitability of the school. She had created zip code maps of both Swallow Hill concertgoers and school attendees, which showed that the concertgoers came from all across the metropolitan area, while students were drawn from the immediate area within a mile or two of the South Pearl Street neighborhood. Maintaining some kind of local presence would be critical to maintaining school revenue, which would be vital to ongoing operations. Flash wasn't everything.

Not many performers can claim they have been at it since the folk scare of the 1960s. Chris Smither was there at the beginning. His riveting guitar work and singing are Denver favorites, whether he's singing an original like "Train Home" or covering Bob Dylan's "Desolation Row." *Swallow Hill Music Association.*

It didn't take Daniels long to see the wisdom in Harry's and Becky's points of view. The traffic and parking issues would make it nearly impossible for students and concertgoers. After all, who would want their kids dragging their guitars to and from class while dodging traffic on the busy one-way main arteries of Broadway and Lincoln? And the area clearly was not in keeping with the friendly neighborhood vision embodied at Pearl Street. The search continued.

But the model that the church represented became a clear guidepost: when it came to their basic design and plan, old churches had exactly what Swallow Hill could use. Daniels and others were convinced that the right church building could make a workable new home, but other recent developments did nothing to encourage them.

Fundraising remained central to Swallow Hill's problems since it would not likely be able to depend on operating revenue alone to cover its expenses. Chris secured concert sponsorship from Wild Oats Market and the Pearl Street Grill and general sponsorship from Schumacher Accounting. Recognizing that its main business model was the Chicago Old Town School of Folk Music, he contacted the school's director, Jim Hirsch, in order to learn more about its operating practices. He discovered that the City of Chicago was far more supportive of its institution than Denver was of Swallow Hill. In 1994, the City of Chicago had donated the abandoned forty-three-thousand-square-foot Hild Library building in one of Chicago's most diverse neighborhoods to the Old Town School. In addition, Chicago corporations provided strong, ongoing financial support.

Daniels believed Swallow Hill needed a new business plan with an emphasis on fundraising and community outreach. He had no experience in the former, so he set about educating himself through reading and meeting with community and business leaders. His self-education led him to understand one of the reasons Swallow Hill's capital campaign had failed to generate much enthusiasm: for its entire existence, Swallow Hill's board of directors neither contributed to the capital campaign nor solicited contributions. In Chris's words, it was not a giving board, and his first step toward successful fundraising was his confrontation with the board over its demonstrated lack of commitment. He contended that if the board did not feel compelled to contribute, how could they expect others to make financial commitments?

By good chance, Chris met Frank Isenhart, co-founder of Tempest, Isenhart, Chafee, Lansdowne & Associates. At the time, Isenhart's investment company was producing a biographical film on Denver jazz impresario Dave Gibson and needed a homey place to film interviews. A friend suggested he contact Swallow Hill. Daniels met Isenhart at the Pearl Street facility, which he showed to Isenhart, who felt it was the perfect setting for filming the interviews. Chris agreed to make the space available. Upon learning about Swallow Hill, Isenhart was so impressed that he immediately took out a membership. After learning about the organizational dilemma, he introduced Daniels to a top-notch business consultant who, at that time, had been working with General Electric. The consultant taught Chris that a key element of business planning was that the best business plan is worthless if the management team does not buy into it. He set out to get buy-in to his plan that included a new building.

Chris did something no one had done before: he initiated a mailing campaign to Swallow Hill's members asking them what *they* wanted most from the organization. What priorities did they place on the school? On concerts? Was one more important than the other? What about location and setting? The members responded that they wanted a place that retained the warm friendliness of Pearl Street and that both the school and concerts were equally important. Armed with that information, Chris engineered an off-site meeting hosted at Isenhart's house, with school director Becky Miklitch, concert director Meredith Carson and board member Larry Fish in attendance. That meeting helped to heal some of the schism between Becky and Meredith, the two most important staff members, and brought Larry firmly into Chris's support group. Chris then approached the board and convinced it to fund a workshop/seminar on organization management presented by Jim Hirsch, the director of the Old Town School of Folk Music. The reasoning was simple: Old Town was the only organization that closely resembled Swallow Hill, and Hirsch had been successful there. Perhaps they could learn from him and his experience. Hirsch is a driven, charismatic and opinionated man; he can polarize people. But he also had the type of experience Swallow Hill could use to its advantage, and the meeting helped to spell out the organizational requirements and business strategies that would move the organization forward. The meeting produced a clear consensus from both staff and board.

Chris's efforts began to bear fruit. The board began to change its focus, and its president, Steve Gavan, voiced solid support for Daniels's new directions. Other board members began to come around, especially Robert Hickler, James Martin and Bob Ambrosius, who put their full support behind Chris's call for a giving board.

When the capital campaign director unexpectedly resigned, Chris agreed to manage that function. Under Seth Weisberg, Swallow Hill had received not one but three prestigious El Pomar awards for excellence. Taking its name from Spanish for "the orchard," Spencer and Julie Penrose had established the El Pomar Foundation in 1937 "to enhance, encourage and promote the current and future well-being of the people of Colorado through grant making and community stewardship." El Pomar contributes $20 million annually to support nonprofit organizations devoted to serving Colorado communities. Chris believed that the time was ripe to approach El Pomar for a grant for additional operating funds. When he was successful, he made grant writing a central part of the organization's efforts. Swallow Hill volunteer Susan Dimichalis, who wrote grants for the Colorado Chorale, reviewed and edited his work. Chris caught on quickly. Armed with excellent writing skills learned as a graduate history student, he hit his stride: he approached the Coors Foundation and Gates Foundation and secured additional grants from both.

Earlier, the SCFD charges that Swallow Hill was "too white" had hurt Seth Weisberg considerably; to counter the SCFD, Chris enlisted Julie Davis, longtime Swallow Hill music instructor, to create the Swallow Hill Traveling Troupe, an outreach effort that visited schools throughout the metro area, bringing music and culture to a large number of children not otherwise exposed to folk music. Swallow Hill received the Denver Mayor's Award for Cultural Excellence and, shortly thereafter, the Colorado Governor's Award for Cultural Excellence. With the success of its community outreach programs, Swallow Hill was able to request and secure new and expanded annual SCFD funding, which provided $35,000 for the production and continuation of outreach educational programs. Over time, Daniels was able to build up a "war chest" of $60,000, with the idea that it might come in handy for expansion.

Still, economic challenges remained. The annual budget in 1996 was more than $300,000, and space remained at a premium. The board, while more receptive to many of Daniels's ideas, was not yet ready to abandon the Pearl Street expansion project, but no other alternatives seemed reasonable.

IF THESE WALLS COULD SPEAK

In 1997, when it seemed likely that the board would move on the expansion project, an alternative appeared almost out of nowhere. Chris received a fax from a realtor offering a church for sale on East Yale Avenue, about a mile from Swallow Hill. Chris took Meredith and Becky to investigate. The property was on the northwest corner of East Yale and Lincoln Avenues and had previously been the home of the Southside Church of the Nazarene. The congregation built the original structure in 1941 and expanded it to its present size in 1953. The church community had remained vital into the 1980s, a time when a young and dynamic pastor led it. When he left in the early '90s to direct a church in California, the church community lost much of its vigor, and its parishioners drifted away to other newer Nazarene communities in the Denver area. The church building was vacant, the parish unable to maintain mortgage payments or meet ongoing maintenance expenses.

Carson and Miklitch were impressed with the property; it had everything they needed. Becky saw that the building was about twenty thousand square feet, nearly ten times what was available at Pearl Street and three times more than what the expansion plan would provide, so there would be more than adequate instruction space. Meredith saw that there were three potential performance spaces that could accommodate between seventy and three hundred concertgoers. There was an area the church had used for Sunday school that would make ideal classroom space, and the original building to the rear of the main building had more than sufficient office space. And there was a paved parking lot across Yale and Lincoln to the southeast; the building was far enough away from Broadway that noise would not be an issue. Chris was not immediately impressed, thinking that it did not have the appeal of a LoDo site. Meredith and Becky won him over with their enthusiasm.

As good as the building appeared, the board was initially torn by the new opportunity. It had grown somewhat attached to the idea of expansion, and here was a building in the general neighborhood that was more than adequate, but the asking price of $650,000 was intimidating. How could Swallow Hill pay for such a place? According to Daniels, board member Bob Ambrosius went to investigate. With his extensive knowledge of real estate, he compared the purchase price to other commercial properties and to the proposed expansion. Ambrosius concluded that the church was a bargain. He pushed the board to act and make a commitment to the property. It resisted. Members did not believe they could manage the financial commitment. Daniels believed otherwise, and Seth Weisberg, a trusted advisor, encouraged Chris to commit to the goal.

Chris acted quickly to reenergize the capital campaign. His father put him in contact with people who had raised money for a community arts center in South Carolina, where Daniels's parents were living. Chris contacted the

Located at 71 East Yale Avenue since 1998, Swallow Hill Music Association continues the traditions established by Harry Tuft and the Denver Folklore Center. *Swallow Hill Music Association.*

RootsFest moved to Denver's recently restored historic Paramount Theater in 2011. *Swallow Hill Music Association.*

Daniels Hall, the largest of Swallow Hill's three performance spaces, comfortably accommodates 340 listeners. *Swallow Hill Music Association.*

Swallow Hill's Tuft Hall is a more intimate performance space, where one hundred concertgoers can see a variety of local and national performers. *Swallow Hill Music Association.*

Right: Local band Paper Bird combines guitars, banjos and brass with eclectic songwriting and infectious harmonies. *Swallow Hill Music Association.*

Below: The late Chet Atkins called Pat Donahue "one of the greatest fingerpickers in the world." He was right. Most people know him for his work on National Public Radio's *A Prairie Home Companion. Swallow Hill Music Association.*

Left: Tom Rush came out of the Boston/Cambridge folk scene and was the first to record songs by Joni Mitchell and James Taylor. He remains a Swallow Hill favorite. *Swallow Hill Music Association*.

Below: Graham Nash and David Crosby wowed the sold-out crowd at Rootsfest with a stunning two-and-a-half-hour-long show that left people grinning ear-to-ear. *Swallow Hill Music Association*.

Local girl Judy Collins headlined RootsFest in 2010 and returned for another sold-out show in 2011. *Swallow Hill Music Association.*

Alt-country singer/songwriter Neko Case showed off her smoky vocals at RootsFest in 2010. *Swallow Hill Music Association.*

World music has a home at Swallow Hill, where Iraq-born Rahim Alhaj (oud) and Indian-born Ali Khan Amjad (sarod) are among the eclectic artists who have appeared there.

The mysterious Leon Redbone brought his gravelly baritone, first-rate fingerpicking, eclectic musical tastes and ever-present shades to Daniels Hall in 2010. *Swallow Hill Music Association.*

Michael Schenkelberg, director of the Julie Davis School of Music at Swallow Hill, taught the Biggest (almost) Guitar Lesson at Denver's Red Rocks Amphitheater in 2008. *Swallow Hill Music Association.*

Denver-born Corey Harris combines the raw emotion of the Delta blues with the influences of Africa and the Caribbean into a unique musical style. *Swallow Hill Music Association.*

The regal Elizabeth Cotton sitting in the Denver Folklore Center before a performance. A deft left-handed guitar player, Cotton worked as a maid for Charles Seeger and cared for his children, Mike and Peggy, who learned her fingerpicking technique. She composed the folk classic "Freight Train." *Larry Schirkey.*

Harry Tuft at the Denver Folklore Center on South Pearl Street in 2005, playing the 1960s vintage Guild guitar that was once owned and used by beloved bluesman Mississippi John Hurt. *Swallow Hill Music Association.*

Texan Guy Clark is one of the most respected songwriters in the world. He doesn't just write them, he crafts them. He also made the guitar he's holding in this picture. A true Renaissance man. *Swallow Hill Music Association.*

manager and asked permission to "appropriate" the design the center had used for its brochure and received unqualified permission. But to kick the campaign off, to prime the pump, Swallow Hill needed a lead grant. Daniels approached his parents, who generously provided a $125,000 donation. With its lead grant in hand, Swallow Hill designed and printed its brochure and kicked off the capital campaign.

At the same time, Daniels and Ambrosius put together a financial plan that demonstrated that the ongoing costs of the leases on Pearl Street and Jewell Avenue for additional classrooms and office space, coupled with performance hall rentals needed for concerts, would be offset through the purchase of the church. Swallow Hill's 1998 operating budget was a projected $600,000. Ultimately, Daniels and Ambrosius were able to convince the board that the move made good economic sense and that they could raise the necessary funds for the down payment and ongoing debt service.

With the commitment of the initial donation, Frank Isenhart put Daniels in touch with "all the right people" at the Coors Foundation, the Gates Foundation and other leading charitable groups, and the capital campaign gathered momentum. Perceiving the possibilities, the board committed to the new building, made the $50,000 down payment from the war chest and moved forward with the purchase.

While the plan to expand Pearl Street appeared more elegant to some, as Daniels put it, the purchase of the church was more practical, but the building required much work before they would be able to occupy it. There was an open-air courtyard at the entrance, which Chris decided should be filled in. Gerry McCallum and Chris led a team of volunteers who filled in the area, placed a roof over it and spread and finished yards of concrete to create a foyer where people could gather before concerts and artists could sell their CDs. McCallum, Swallow Hill's volunteer coordinator, was tireless. He organized gangs to attack the plumbing, the electrical work and the roofing, refurbishing or replacing defective materials. Member and musician Rich Moore, Molly O'Brien's husband, was the owner of a heating company, and he inspected the furnace and found that not only did it not meet code but also it was downright dangerous. Moore agreed to refurbish the clunky unit at cost.

Swallow Hill scheduled its annual Folkathon to coincide with the grand opening of the new facility. While the name "folkathon" was Harry Tuft's idea, the concept came from board members in 1992. The original idea was to present a weekend-long, around-the-clock celebration of folk music and dance, featuring the finest in local talent. The goals were simple: offer Denver citizens unique and memorable summer entertainment that would raise funds and create greater interest in Swallow Hill Music Association. The first musician to play the original Folkathon was Bob Tyler, who penned the "Folkathon Theme Song." The event included food and craft vendors, children's games, all-night jam sessions and dance demonstrations on multiple stages. At the old facility, the city had given Swallow Hill

Born in West Virginia, brother and sister Tim and Molly O'Brien have been fixtures on the Denver music scene for years. Tim worked at the DFC while he honed his chops and was a founding member of the bluegrass band Hot Rize. Molly and her husband, guitarist Rich Moore, regularly perform at Swallow Hill. *Swallow Hill Music Association.*

permission to block off sections of Pearl Street and Jewell Avenue to create a street fair that had been quite successful, and the neighborhood stood solidly behind it. But the new facility straddled two municipalities—Denver and Englewood—and its new neighbors were somewhat suspicious about such a gathering. The plan called for an outdoor main stage on Lincoln Avenue adjacent to Swallow Hill, with other performance stages inside, while food vendors plied their wares on Lincoln. But to get ready, Daniels felt that they would need to refurbish the floor of the main concert hall, which was covered in dingy industrial carpet. Volunteers removed the old carpet only to find inches-thick layers of carpet glue on top of the old hardwood floor, which would require hand stripping. With his so-so Spanish, Chris went to Labor Ready and hired a crew of Spanish-speaking workers to strip the glue from the floor. After instructing the workers, Daniels removed himself to his office to tackle a waiting mound of paperwork. The Folkathon was just two days away, and there was much to be done. The workers decided that a little water might just do the trick in loosening the glue. Without asking permission, they brought in a hose from outside and flooded the floor. When Daniels took a break from his work, he found, to his dismay, the workers happily scraping away at the glue, now covered in an inch or so of water. "No agua! No agua!" he shouted excitedly. He turned the water off and scoured the facility for towels, cloths, paper towels and even toilet paper—anything to soak up the water. They finally brought in a fan and dried the floor for twenty-four hours. To his relief, the wooden floorboards did not warp, and the hall was ready for the crowds the following day. The Folkathon was another success, with Chris Daniels and his band, the Kings, closing the show with an energetic horn-soaked set in the early evening.

Swallow Hill moved into its new building after the Folkathon. True to form, Becky set up the classrooms, helped create new offerings and filled the classes. Meredith had three halls at her disposal in the new building: the Café, which would hold about 60 people; Tuft Hall (named, appropriately, for Harry Tuft), which seated 100 comfortably; and the main performance area, Daniels Hall, which could accommodate 340. (Daniels's parents had wanted the hall to be named for their son, but Chris demurred, sensing that it might appear to be too egotistical; he did, however, agree to have it named for his family.) Meredith could book acts—both local and national—without leasing performance spaces, except in rare instances when the artist was sure to draw more than 350 fans. Chris Daniels and his band donated the PA system, which Swallow Hill professionally installed in the main hall, running the cabling from the stage under the floor to the sound board in the rear and mounting the speakers in a way that took advantage of the room's natural acoustics. Artists frequently comment on Swallow Hill's good sound and attentive audiences.

The new building brought Daniels and Swallow Hill new opportunities and new challenges. With the improved performance space came increased notoriety: artists wanted to play Swallow Hill but now felt they could ask for larger performance fees. Swallow Hill also had to be more diligent in tracking and paying performance royalties to ASCAP (the American Society of Composers, Authors and Publishers) and BMI (Broadcast Music, Inc.), the largest companies that manage publication and performance copyright in America. Even though Swallow Hill no longer paid out money to rent performance space, the cost of presenting concerts rose, putting financial pressure on the organization and the budget.

Daniels believed that, in order to better serve local musicians, Swallow Hill should have a recording studio where musicians might record their work without spending excessive sums of money. Charlie Sawtelle, the outstanding guitarist from the nationally known bluegrass band Hot Rize, had recently passed away after years of battling cancer, and Chris approached Sawtelle's family and convinced them to donate the professional-grade recording equipment that Charlie had previously installed in his private home studio. His family agreed, and in return, Swallow Hill named the studio after this outstanding—and much missed—bluegrass guitarist. The Sawtelle Studio now occupies rooms in the basement of Swallow Hill.

Chris continued to manage the capital campaign and set a goal of $800,000, believing that it would require that amount to reduce the organization's debt load, refurbish the building and keep a reasonable cash reserve. By 2000, the campaign had managed to collect $680,000, a significant success for an organization that had started with no fundraising skills. Swallow Hill's operating budget continued to grow as well. When Chris took over the executive director's position in 1996, the operating budget had stood at a little more than $300,000. It had increased to nearly $600,000 in 1998 and approached $1,000,000 in 2000. The effort required to continually find additional funding was beginning to take its toll.

By early 2000, Chris Daniels began feeling burned out. He had made, he thought, a significant contribution, but the pay, even though it had increased to $40,000 per year, was still a bit low considering the number of hours the position required. Chris Daniels and the Kings had continued to play 130 shows a year and were experiencing renewed popularity. One day, Daniels ran into blues musician and friend Mary Flower in the hallway outside his office at Swallow Hill, and Mary said, "You look like shit, Chris." He had to agree, and after discussions with his wife, he decided it was time to resign.

The board reluctantly accepted his resignation and set about looking for a suitable replacement.

Characterizing Daniels's tenure as executive director is not simple. The numbers tell only part of the story, but an essential part nonetheless. Daniels was executive director from 1995 until 2000. The annual budget grew from $300,000 to nearly $1,000,000; membership grew from 1,800 to more than 2,500; teachers from 22 to 35; and students from 1,500 to more than 2,600. Daniels engineered the search for a new building, initiated a successful capital campaign and moved Swallow Hill into a twenty-thousand-square-foot facility. One might say that it was not a bad run for a rock-and-roll bandleader with no formal business education.

But that represents only part of what he accomplished, and not the accomplishments of which he is most proud. In an interview in 2005, when asked what he considered his most important accomplishments, his first response came quickly: Daniels was delighted by Swallow Hill's continued emphasis on excellence in all its programs. And while he was proud of the fundraising success, he took greater pride in Swallow Hill having presented the first Acoustic Blues Festival west of the Mississippi and the creation of Swallow Hill's Traveling Troupe. He was pleased to have been able to move the board toward a more business-like environment and getting it to come around to believing that it needed to lead fundraising through its own giving. His eyes reflected his enthusiasm for taking ideas from nowhere and making them work, but he was quick to credit the volunteers who made it happen. If Daniels's leadership had a slogan, it was, "Okay, this is gonna work!" Rebecca Miklitch stated that it was Daniels's enthusiasm and energy that frequently carried the day and got people to believe they could reach their goals.

Amidst the obvious plusses, there were disappointments and failures. Daniels reflected that he never fully resolved the conflicts between Miklitch and Carson, noting that Becky clung to the profit center concept and that the concerts never made much money, not even in the new building, where costs should have been lower but were not. And by his own admission, he never fully changed the dysfunction of the board of directors, which used to meet mostly to discuss folk music rather than address Swallow Hill's business and organizational needs. When he left, the capital campaign had "only" taken in $680,000 against its $800,000 goal.

When asked why he ever wanted the job in the first place, Chris quietly responded that he simply thought he could make a difference. He didn't come in with a definite set of goals, but he felt strongly that he could help

A master of both the six- and twelve-string blues guitar (not to mention harmonica), Paul Geremia has been a serious student of the blues since the 1960s. He spices his shows with stories of the bluesmen and women he knew during the 1960s folk revival and has influenced many of the younger generation of upcoming players.

the organization. "I felt that I could make a difference in the way Swallow Hill perceived itself. Until Seth, they saw themselves always as struggling; then they hit a wall." When he left, the board elegantly and succinctly summed up Daniels's contribution by saying that he had pulled them all through a knothole.

Chris believes he got a lot more out of his experience than he gave. He pointed to his band's CD *Louie, Louie*, which he believes grew from his time at Swallow Hill. Another CD, *The Spark*, released in 2003, a few years after he left, reflects his reattraction to acoustic music. He fondly remembered three shows presented during his tenure: French finger-style guitarist Pierre Bensusan at Cameron Church ("I was knocked out! How can anyone play that well?"); local singer/songwriter Chuck Pyle, with Gordon Burt on fiddle, at the old Swallow Hill ("His songwriting is so tight and his guitar playing unique."); and playing the then newly named Daniels Hall with the Kings ("And beaming because the room sounded so good!"). When he visited Swallow Hill in 2004, he was delighted to find his old couch in the area backstage. "It's like a piece of me is there for all the performers," he said. "But you know, I'm really glad of one thing. I'm proud we never sold the naming rights to one of the halls. We named it Tuft Hall. That was the right thing to do." And that might summarize Chris Daniels's time as Swallow Hill's executive director: he did the right thing for Swallow Hill.

7

A CHANGE IS GONNA COME

The board hired Jim Williams to replace Chris Daniels in 2000. Like other comings and goings, it marked the end of one era and the beginning of another. Swallow Hill faced some of the same issues it always had—money—plus new challenges as it strove to keep itself fresh and relevant. Williams was a good find.

Jim Williams wears his long graying hair pulled back in a ponytail. His eyes give his face the wise but sad appearance of an uncle who might have played in a rock band in the 1960s. He was born in 1945 in Beaumont, Texas; his father was of Scotch-Irish descent, and his mother, a Christian fundamentalist, was part Cherokee. Listening to and making music, both religious and secular, formed an important part of his family life. Growing up in east Texas and Louisiana, he heard a gumbo mixture of Cajun and zydeco music, with a strong dose of the blues spun into the mix. (Zydeco is an accordion-based musical genre that originated in south central and southwest Louisiana, the music of the Creoles of Color, who borrowed many of its defining elements from Cajun music.)

As a teenager too young to drink in Texas, Jim and his friends visited the clubs in south Louisiana, where liquor was available and the music was a loud concoction of rhythm and blues and blue-eyed soul. After attending a stifling freshman year on a football scholarship at Abilene Christian College ("a disaster; too restrictive; it was a strict fundamentalist school"), he transferred to Lamar Tech in Beaumont for a semester and then finished his education at the University of Houston, graduating in 1967 with a degree in research psychology. After graduation, he did some computer programming

Mance Lipscomb was one of a number of bluesmen "rediscovered" during the folk revival in the 1960s. Like Mississippi John Hurt, he had been a farmer living far from the stage. He was an outstanding musician who read music and played everything from blues to pop to ballads and spirituals. *Larry Schirkey.*

at the National Aeronautics and Space Administration (NASA).

He worked his way through the university as a chauffeur for an oil pipeline company; he was the only white chauffeur on the staff but struck a close bond with the other drivers, who welcomed him into their social group. His fellow drivers introduced him to country blues, taking him to the then mostly black juke joints to hear such greats as Lightning Hopkins and Mance Lipscomb. It was a world of difference from Beaumont, where in the 1960s schools and society were still very much segregated.

During college, Williams worked a few summers at a liberal Christian youth camp in New Jersey, funded by Clinton Davidson, a wealthy insurance man. Somehow, his work there earned him a divinity deferment from the Selective Service, considerably fortunate in the midst of the Vietnam War when every male over eighteen was eligible for military service. Jim and others from the camp proposed a new program to Davidson that would recruit volunteers who would dedicate a year to working with disadvantaged kids in New York City ghettos. The idea was that the volunteers would raise their own funds and had to live on less than $300 a month.

From 1967 to 1971, Jim and his wife lived in a sixth-floor walk-up in the Tremont section of the Bronx, where they were responsible for early childhood education programs. He and his co-workers were white, and while living in the Bronx, they were "the only white faces within twenty blocks." He also received training as a "corporation founder," part of

President Johnson's War on Poverty and Model Cities programs, which were spending millions in American ghettos in a noble, if failed, effort to eradicate poverty. His main job was to find community leaders and help them set up nonprofit corporations that would receive federal funds for day care, housing, arts and crafts, recreation and music. Part of his fundraising efforts had Williams organizing rock concerts of mostly local bands, which taught him some of the fundamentals of music promotion. While in New York, his wife earned her master's in education from New York University, and Jim studied urban planning.

After four difficult years, burned out from job stress and living in poverty, they moved to Nashville, Tennessee, where Jim had his first exposure to the country music of the Grand Ole Opry:

> *We hung out at Roy Acuff's studios and met lots of people. Saw the recording process where Acuff's famous rule of thumb was: do it in one take. I took in lots of music at local clubs: the Old Time Pickin' Parlor, Bluebird Café, the Exit Inn. My buddy Roy and I would carry empty guitar cases around to the stage door of clubs, including the Ryman Auditorium, home of the Grand Ole Opry and walk in and hang out backstage. I just wanted to see what it was all about from a musician's point of view. I met Norman Blake* [outstanding guitar/Dobro/banjo player], *who held court at the Old Time Pickin' Parlor, where his title was president of the "Dobrolic Plectoral Society." All the great players from the Ryman came by. It was my intro to Appalachian-based music.*

Having spent a few years in Nashville, the Williamses became caught up in the alternative lifestyle movement. They sold everything they owned, bought a pickup truck with a camper and moved to Eugene, Oregon, where they lived for twelve years. Eugene was, at the time, "the most experimental place on the West Coast; everyone was there: the Grateful Dead, Jackson Browne, Joni Mitchell." He worked at a mental health center and then became involved in the creation of the Woodmen of the World (WOW) Hall, a nonprofit organization somewhat similar to Swallow Hill.

The Woodmen is a fraternal organization founded in Omaha by Joseph Cullen Root in 1890. Today, it is a large financial services organization. Its building in Eugene was originally a Presbyterian church built in 1906. The Woodmen of the World purchased the building and renamed it. In 1932, WOW replaced it with the present building, and in the late 1970s, local musicians banded together to buy the hall, raising $10,000 in just one week. "Just a bunch of old hippies who had no money themselves, but we presented a twenty-three-hour marathon where some three hundred musicians played one set after the other. It's still there." As its first executive director, Jim booked acts, including autoharpist extraordinaire Bryan Bowers, folk singer Tom Rush and the rocking Paul Butterfield Blues Band.

It was at this time—the mid- to late '70s—when many organizations like Swallow Hill and WOW came into being. Counterculture people and antiwar activists who never exactly went along with the cultural mainstream and retained much of their 1960s idealism created new cultural organizations. One of them was in Oregon. "The Oregon County Fair—it's sorta Woodstock meets Swallow Hill—came into being. It was crafts, a collective and camping on a one-thousand-acre festival site, featuring all handmade goods. Kinda like the Renaissance Festival in Larkspur."

He was also involved in founding the Eugene Performing Arts Center. "I was on the commission that raised the $20 million bonds and designed the building, with a 2,500-seat room and a 500-seat room, on two city blocks. I was the production coordinator during its first three years." Then, for five years, he was the cultural arts director for Austin, Texas, and then worked as a cultural exchange consultant for the Netherlands government. Figuring he could perform consulting from almost anywhere, he moved to the mountains between Albuquerque and Santa Fe, New Mexico. He then became the director of the New Mexico Jazz Workshop until the end of 1999.

THIS LITTLE TOWN

Williams claims he heard about the position opening at Swallow Hill by word of mouth and initially had no real interest, but then he decided to "pop a résumé in the mail." Swallow Hill board member Judith Pierson invited him to interview with the whole board of directors. And he talked with Chris Daniels. "I liked the extended family of Swallow Hill but was not particularly attracted to living in the city." In the end, he accepted the position as Swallow Hill's executive director.

There was little in the way of formal transition between Daniels and Williams:

It was a troubled first year, with lots of financial problems. Swallow Hill had not figured out the costs of operating the new building, which required many improvements. We were in the red. And I had to learn about the school operation but relied on Becky, who had great experience. The school was making money, but the rest of the operation was not. We had to get a handle on spending. We had to reduce staff.

With the concerts losing money, Jim asked Meredith Carson to resign. Relying on his long experience booking shows, he assumed the duties of concert director in order to save Swallow Hill the cost of a separate position. Budget restraints also led to other staff reductions. It was painful, but it had a stabilizing impact on finances, although it did not address revenue growth.

In 2004, Swallow Hill was able to move into Scientific and Cultural Facilities Tax District (SCFD) tier two, which added substantially to its annual funding. It was a crucial turning point. With dependable funding, Swallow Hill could plan for the future in a way not previously possible. Tier two provided more funding for general operating support rather than specific project-related funding, and for the first time, Swallow Hill could establish better staff at better pay.

Jim contended that Denver was different from the Northeast, where he believed there was a greater tradition of supporting the arts and culture, citing, for example, the City of Chicago giving a building to the Old Town School of Folk Music. "And there are companies and individuals more inclined to give. And states provide funds; Colorado did not initially do that. But SCFD funding changed that." Williams believed that Swallow Hill provided Denver and Colorado with a special service: "It preserves and presents not only touring artists but local artists who represent local culture [cowboy, Latino, et cetera]."

And he also believed that it goes beyond culture:

Let me tell you a story. A fellow in his mid-fifties showed up one evening wearing a business suit, with his daughter. They were both carrying fiddle cases. Out of curiosity, I asked them why they were here. The man said that their family had been in trouble. They needed a way to communicate, so he and his daughter were taking Irish fiddle lessons. Together. That's part of the uniqueness of Swallow Hill; it can do something most other cultural organizations can't do.

But challenges remained. For Swallow Hill to remain in SCFD tier two beyond 2009, it would have to increase its annual revenue by $250,000, and increasing revenue and attracting and maintaining—and paying—quality staff was Jim's biggest concern. Concerts and the school represented equal

A young singer gets his chance at the mic. Michael Schenkelberg (far left) has continued Swallow Hill's community outreach with its Traveling Troupe that takes music to schools. *Swallow Hill Music Association.*

revenue streams, netting about the same each year. Jim believed that they achieved the balance through increased quantity, developing target (i.e., repeat) audiences and raising ticket prices to a more realistic level. Under his leadership, Swallow Hill launched its first website and then improved it so that it would allow patrons to book classes and purchase tickets online, thus holding down operating expenses.

If there was a weakness in Denver, Jim believed it was the lack of local media support for cultural organizations like Swallow Hill. Local NPR outlets (KCFR and KVOD) focused more on news and classical music, respectively; they saw no place in their programming for synergy with Swallow Hill and its community. More broadly, consolidation in media ownership had hamstrung local commercial radio. Stations were no longer locally owned or programmed; only the bottom line mattered anymore. With the exception of KGNU, no local stations presented the music of—let alone conversations with—artists who performed at Swallow Hill. Williams said:

> *I believe you are what you eat. If you don't get to hear some of this music, you never develop a taste for it. And none of it gets played locally. How are you going to develop a love for it? It is a self-fulfilling prophecy. Radio*

Music is just as much for kids as it is for adults, maybe more. Swallow Hill provides a wide array of class offerings for children of all ages.

programmers believe if you don't hear the music, people must not like it. Radio stations today are all about making money, which means getting listeners and advertisers. Most stations do not have a program manager. The music is beamed in via satellite. They have a receptionist and a sales staff, neither of which can tell you what music is on the air. They only know the Arbitron ratings. The Internet may represent our best chance to get on the air.

Jim wanted to reach out to other ethnic communities:

Swallow Hill is seen as part of the white suburbs, and blacks and Latinos generally do not accept it. Most of the Latino music presented at Swallow Hill, for example, has crossed over to a white audience. The same is true for blues. We need to find a way to reach out and include non-white audiences. What I learned from living in the ghetto in New York City is that you don't do something to people, you do it with them. Swallow Hill needs to do the same somehow.

At a time when most nonprofits were earning 50 percent or more of their annual income from public donations, Swallow Hill was doing better, relying on public funding for just 35 percent of its annual income. Still, the organization faced many challenges, including learning how to leverage its political advantage and how to grow the business. Williams hit on one idea: getting Swallow Hill out in front of a great number of people by taking concerts outside the walls of Yale Avenue and into larger venues. It was a gamble. No one knew if it would pay off.

8

THE FUTURE'S SO BRIGHT

Just as Jim Williams had thrown out the gambit to "go bigger," he announced his intentions to step down as executive director, hoping he might stay on as concert director. The board of directors initiated what turned out to be a rather long and laborious seven-month search for a replacement. There was no lack of interest on the part of applicants, but the board was more selective this time than ever before. It made it clear that it wanted someone who was dynamic, a leader, someone with business leadership experience as well as concert promotion. It wanted all this but at no significant increase in pay. What were the board members thinking? As it turned out, the next executive director was out there in Swallow Hill's Denver community. He had taken guitar lessons occasionally at Swallow Hill but had attended few of its concerts.

When the search kicked off, Tom Scharf was the successful owner and manager of Scharf's Services, a Denver advertising company. He lived reasonably comfortably, was married with a three-year-old son and was not really looking for a new job opportunity. Still, he admitted that there was something going on that he could not quite put his finger on at the time—some small bit of restlessness had invaded his life.

Tom was born in Albuquerque, New Mexico, in 1962 and moved to the state capital of Santa Fe when he was two years old. His father was a surgeon and his mother a registered nurse who had retired to stay home and raise her four children. When Tom was just nine years old, his mother passed away suddenly at the age of thirty-four, never having fully recovered from serious neck surgery. Though Tom was just a kid, his mother had already instilled in him a strong musical curiosity, and he eventually took up the old nylon-string classical guitar she had played.

In an unexpected move, Tom's father shifted his medical practice from surgery to psychiatry and secured a position overseeing the New Mexico Behavioral Health Institute in Las Vegas, New Mexico. Dr. Scharf did not think the Las Vegas schools were quite up to the level he wanted for his children, so he arranged for Tom and his siblings to go to high school in Albuquerque. It was there that Tom first encountered acting and singing. Though he had taken a few guitar lessons when he was younger, he was hardly enamored with the instrument, but high school—and rock-and-roll—convinced him to become more interested in unraveling the guitar's mysteries.

After graduation, Tom attended the University of Massachusetts in Boston, where he studied English and political science with an eye toward law school:

> *I was playing music a lot by then and living just a few blocks from Harvard Square. I would sometimes go to the laundromat and put a load of clothes in the washer and start it up, then go out on the sidewalk in front, take out my guitar and leave the case open in front of me and start singing to see if I could make enough cash to pay for the dryer. It usually worked. Then one day, a cop came along and told me that I couldn't be out there playing for money if I didn't have a license. License? How did I know I needed a license? So I went down, stood in line and got a license so I could continue busking. I still have it; it's there on the wall behind my desk* [pointing to it proudly]. *First money I ever made making music.*

He graduated in 1984 with degrees in political science and English and no firm plans for the future. His brother Matt lived in Denver and told him that jobs were available. Tom arrived in Denver ready to start his job search and asked Matt what he should do next. "Let's go hiking," came the answer, so the Scharf brothers spent ten days traipsing about Wyoming's Grand Tetons. The majestic mountains and wilderness hooked him, and he decided Denver might be a good place to live. He's never left.

When it came time to get a bit more serious about looking for work, he landed an acting role at the Country Dinner Playhouse, tended bar for a while and then clerked for a year at a Denver law firm:

> *I had taken English and political science because I thought it would be good preparation for law school. I clerked for a year while preparing for the*

LSAT, which I passed, but that year cleared away any illusions I had about the law. I had visions of Perry Mason and fighting against injustice. Law work turned out to be boring research in dusty books. I was disillusioned.

Matt Scharf, a successful graphics artist, suggested that his own talents and contacts and Tom's flair for writing and salesmanship would make a good pairing for an advertising agency, so they boldly hung out a shingle, and Tom began pitching the company to local businesses. It worked rather well. Within a few years, they were able to count Adolph Coors, USWest, MediaOne and Denver University among their clients. Advertising is a feast-or-famine business, but the brothers were wise enough to salt away their earnings when times were good, and the late 1980s were not bad.

Tragedy struck when Matt suffered serious, life-threatening head injuries in a car accident. A car ran a traffic light and slammed into the 1950s vintage Porsche convertible he was riding in, and his head struck the top of the windscreen. It was touch and go for a while, but Matt survived. After multiple surgeries and rehabilitation, he was ready to return to work but decided he could no longer tolerate Denver's traffic and hustle and bustle, so he packed up his belongings and moved to Steamboat Springs, where he designed and built a home. Remarkably, their business survived. Tom continued to bring in the customers, and using the phone, fax and FedEx, they maintained their successful advertising agency.

In 2007, Scharf learned that Swallow Hill Music Association was looking for a new executive director. Initially, applying seemed out of the question. First in his mind was that the pay was considerably less than what he was pulling down, and the hours were demanding. With a three-year-old son at home, Tom did not want any job that would keep him occupied sixty to seventy hours a week. He remained an avid musician, but the Swallow Hill position did not feel like a good fit at first.

Even before the opportunity arose, he had become restless—or at least open to change. "I'm not a particularly religious person," he said, "and I usually plan things out. I like to set goals and then plan to reach them, especially when it comes to business. For some strange reason—maybe something metaphysical—I had placed an empty manila file folder on my desk and marked it 'My Life.' I'm not sure why I did that, but I felt certain that opportunities, whatever they might be, would come my way." The Swallow Hill opening went into the folder with a few other entries, and he submitted his application even though his heart wasn't in it. At least, not yet.

According to Swallow Hill board member Jim Butler, after searching for seven months there were sixty-five applicants. The board had the responsibility to sort through the applications and narrow it to a working short-list. By that time, Tom had interviewed with a number of board members, including Harry Tuft, whom he had known for years. After much deliberation, the board narrowed it down to its top three candidates and devised a final selection process. Tom said:

> *They invited each of the three candidates to come down to Swallow Hill's Daniels Hall, where we each in turn appeared on stage. Now in previous interviews, I had worn a suit and tie, but this time I dressed appropriately down in jeans and a work shirt. When I saw the setting, I was ready. I had been through dozens of "auditions" before and thought, "Okay, you want a performance?" They gave each candidate about five minutes to explain why they thought they were the right choice for the job. Another thing was that by this time, I wanted the job, and I am competitive. I knew I was right for it and that I had something to give. After my "speech," the board started peppering me with questions, including what it was I was going to do for Swallow Hill. I was calm and I was ready.*

He got the job.

During the drawn-out search process, Tom had slowly warmed to the idea of the job, pay decrease or not, but he harbored no illusions about what lay ahead. Coming into his office the first day, he noticed dishes piled in the kitchen sink and a broken coffee maker sitting on a chair in a dried puddle of coffee. This is unacceptable, he thought. He had always believed that the "experience" of taking lessons or attending a concert at Swallow Hill had been extraordinary. "You get in the door," he said, "and you sense that you are a part of something special. But the environment clearly needed attention. This sort of funkiness did nothing to enrich the experience." He came up with an idea that he admits he might not repeat today, but he prevailed upon the board to enhance the physical environment, asking each board member to "adopt a room." Each would be in charge of a room makeover, repainting it, upgrading the lighting and adding a painting or two. The board, to its credit, bought in. Tom did not exclude himself from the process; he oversaw the straightening of the business offices and refurbishing the flooring. Nothing fancy, mind you, but a clear improvement over the musty seediness that had crept in over the years.

Tom Scharf, a fine guitarist and singer, became Swallow Hill's executive director in 2007 and has led it into a new era of growth. *Swallow Hill Music Association.*

Finances and profitability were a different challenge. He already knew the "big numbers": Swallow Hill's revenues were about $1.2 million. Annual revenue was about equally divided among the school, concerts and SCFD funding grants, but what about expenses? The first two revenue streams— concerts and the school—were essentially break-even ventures at best. More restricting was SCFD funding, which, by design, Swallow Hill could not use for capital expenses. As a result of that restriction, Swallow Hill had performed no capital improvements for seven years, which is to say, the building was falling apart because revenues were never sufficient to keep up. To meet his goal of enhancing the environment, that had to change.

Taking It to the Streets

Tom devised a program—not without risk—that placed Swallow Hill's focus on growth: increase revenue while decreasing dependence on public (i.e., SCFD) support. He realized that public support would always be subject to political whims and in difficult economic times could disappear altogether.

To achieve the desired revenue increase, Scharf called on his marketing and leadership skills. First, more than anything else, Swallow Hill needed to rebrand itself; it was too self-contained. Tom realized that one of Denver's most important cultural organizations was a hidden gem. Nearly everything Swallow Hill did—concerts, lessons, et cetera—happened inside the walls of its East Yale Avenue building. If you weren't a member, a student or an occasional concertgoer, you didn't know about Swallow Hill. He also recognized that annual revenue was uneven. Revenue was strong in the winter when people took lessons and attended concerts, but the summer months were nearly dead since people sought outdoor activities and attended other shows. How to change the perceptions? Tom suggested a plan that would, in his words, "take the mission to the streets."

Swallow Hill had gained experience in open-air shows dating back to its Folkathons on South Pearl Street, and before moving to Yale Avenue, it had presented shows at other venues, notably Cameron Church, when it needed a larger venue. But since moving to its present location, it had increasingly become self-contained, which was good for managing costs but not so good for encouraging growth or gaining a larger public. Scharf credits Jim Williams with the idea of the RootsFest, an annual celebration with a big show in a large Denver venue. In its early days, Swallow Hill had tried—and failed dramatically—to make such shows financially successful, but it took the plunge and booked the first RootsFest in Denver's historic 2,300-seat Ellie Caulkins Theater and contracted bluesman Taj Mahal as its headliner. History seemed to repeat itself when the concert failed to sell out and lost money. More importantly, Swallow Hill demonstrated that it did not know how to pull off a large show; the sound system didn't work for half the performance, and the presentation looked amateurish.

Tom, the optimist, was convinced they could put those lessons to good use. With the ball in his court for the second RootsFest, Swallow Hill booked a number of local supporting acts, plus Nancy Griffith and Canadian singer/songwriter and guitarist extraordinaire Bruce Cockburn, in the same venue. It was determined to build on its experience, and this time it made things work. The show came off without a hitch, and Swallow Hill sold more tickets and came close to breaking even. Each year since then, Swallow Hill has gained experience in both presenting and marketing RootsFest, and in 2011, David Crosby and Graham Nash played to a sold-out Paramount Theater. And Swallow Hill made money.

Concurrently, Swallow Hill took on the responsibility of booking the acts for other civic events, including the Old South Pearl Street BrewGrass Music Festival and the Old South Pearl Street Brews and Blues Fest, two events that have become fixtures on Denver's summer calendar. More recently, Swallow Hill has successfully assumed the booking of all acts—folk and otherwise—for the Denver Botanic Gardens' summer concert series held at that historic location.

By 2011, revenues topped $3.6 million, and SCFD support was down to about 20 percent of total revenue. The financial risk has apparently paid off, and Swallow Hill has significantly raised its public presence in Denver.

Teacher Cameos

While its concert series remains its public face, the Julie Davis School of Music is its soul. Members and nonmembers alike attend concerts at various venues, but school is where people bond in a way that is hard to explain in simple terms.

Long before becoming executive director, Tom Scharf had taken a number of guitar lessons and developed strong feelings about the school, which never seems to garner widespread public attention but has been the organization's mainstay since the beginning. Its more than forty instructors teach more than four thousand students a year, offering everything from voice and piano lessons to guitar, banjo, mandolin and a variety of instruments, stringed or otherwise. Classes range from traditional folk styles—blues, Travis-style guitar and Scruggs-style banjo—to the guitar styles of Led Zeppelin, Jimi Hendrix and Pink Floyd's David Gilmore. Students, who include adults, teens and tots, can choose between private or group lessons. Because of Swallow Hill's strong national reputation, visiting performers often take time to conduct workshops, giving aspiring musicians a chance to experience a master-class musician up close and personal.

Tom hoped to improve the school's efforts by bringing in a different type of teacher. Most of the school's earliest instructors were self-taught musicians who had learned their crafts in a time when formal music instruction was

After each eight-week-long session, classes get the chance to show off what they learned in a graduation performance. Here is one by the School of Rock graduates. *Swallow Hill Music Association.*

largely unavailable. Both locally and nationally, instructors had often learned music and instrumental styles informally, by listening to records, watching performers and swapping ideas and licks with like-minded players. These men and women brought a special passion to music education that stems from their eagerness to share what they know with anyone willing to learn. Denver native and multi-instrumentalist Ernie Martinez is a good example.

Born in 1956, Ernie started his musical education after seeing the movie version of *The Music Man* at age four. His father played guitar, but Ernie was too small for one, so his parents started him on ukulele. "I didn't know about Hawaiian music," he said. "I just knew this was a downsized guitar and learned melodies. Beatles' tunes and whatever was on the radio back then…I pretty much stayed with the uke until I grew into the guitar, but I was actually pretty much a drummer back then."

Ernie took piano lessons and learned to read music, "but I never stuck with it," he said. "I was more of an ear player. I could learn a lot quicker and more efficiently by ear." Because of his impaired vision, Ernie attended a number of different elementary schools—Lincoln, McKinley, Asbury—all of which offered unique programs for the visually impaired. After the sixth grade, he attended regular classes at Denver's Rishel Junior High and then South High School for a year before graduating from Lincoln High School, all the while playing in a variety of bands.

In 1969, another musical wave hit and floored him: he saw *Bonnie and Clyde* at the movies and *Hee Haw* and *The Beverly Hillbillies* on TV. "I got my first huge taste of bluegrass," he recalled.

> *I didn't know what it was exactly until* Deliverance *came out. First, it was the E-minor chord in "Foggy Mountain Breakdown" that caught my ear, then "Dueling Banjos" from* Deliverance. *I was coming home from a movie late one night, and "Dueling Banjos" came on the radio, and I said to my friends, "Shut up! I want to hear this!" And I just glued my attention to the radio. I heard that slow part, but it was once they got into the fast part that I just couldn't believe it. So I just knew I had to learn to play it.*

Can you learn complicated Scruggs-style banjo picking by ear?

> *Well, one of my sisters was dating a Celtic guitarist, Jerry Barlow, and he had just started to play banjo. I listened to him practice, and that propelled me into it more. Then I bought a five-string banjo, and he showed me stuff, but I could actually* hear *those Scruggs rolls and figure them out. It got a little bit easier, but I wore out a lot of records putting them down to 16rpm, which is an octave lower than at 33rpm, but it helped me learn that style. It just got easier and more fun, and that led me to the mandolin, and then back to guitar bluegrass style. And then Dobro.*

That brought to his mind his first time at the Denver Folklore Center. His cousin, Joe Zambrano, a music critic for the *Denver Post*, took him to the first open mic he ever did:

> *It was early in 1973, and Joe and I did a bit together, him on guitar and me on banjo. After that, we formed a band with some buddies and took a bunch of Flatt and Scruggs and Dillards tunes, and we learned as much as we could. After that first time at the Folklore Center, I was hooked, and later on, Joe introduced me to Dave Ferretta's Global Village. I ended up knowing Dave pretty well and ended up working at his store. And we played at Sweet Loretta's. And at that time there was the band, City Limits, with banjoist Lynn Morris.*

It was Lynn who got Ernie into teaching banjo: "I started teaching banjo in the late 1970s when I filled in for her at the Folklore Center when she would be booked playing. After she left town, I just took over her position. I used to go down to the store and hang out and play instruments and meet all the people."

Ernie didn't get to know Harry Tuft until after Harry reopened the DFC in 1992. Martinez remembered:

We knew each other, but not really well. I also taught at Gordon Close's Melody Music for a couple of years, and Harry used to come in during the early 1980s, but we didn't get to know each other until he opened the store again. I was on hiatus from Swallow Hill at the time, and when he reopened the DFC on Pearl Street, I started going in there all the time.

Ernie didn't have much to do with Swallow Hill, having left teaching in 1981 to pursue other work. He joined a touring country band in 1994, but

when it got off the road, he needed work and one day received a call from Becky Miklitch inquiring if he was interested in a teaching position. "I had to go and audition for it, but that's okay. So in 1995, I was back there. And I'll stay there as long as I can. It's such a fun place."

Ernie's musical career spans more than three decades, and he has become Denver's go-to guy for his versatility and reliability. He has played with nearly everyone on the Denver music scene, though he is perhaps best known as Jon Chandler's guitar and mandolin player. Ernie met Chandler, a local singer/

Denver-born Ernie Martinez might be the ultimate sideman: if it has strings on it, he can play it. And he's a pretty fair teacher as well. But then, so are all the fine musicians who lead classes at Swallow Hill's Julie Davis School of Music. *Swallow Hill Music Association.*

122

songwriter, in 1993, when Ernie's band brought Jon in to Kerr-Macey Studios to do the vocal tracks on a demo recording. "We hit it off right away. I could see the power of Jon's vocals and his tremendous harmonica playing. We started gigging immediately." Chandler plays a monthly songwriters' circle at Kit Simon's Olde Town Pickin' Parlor in Arvada, where Jon plays host to two other area singer/songwriters, showcasing their talents in a small, intimate setting. Ernie provides stellar guitar and mandolin back up.

As a teacher, Ernie has been able to dissect all the musical complexities and boil them down into bite-sized chunks for beginners or force-feed Scruggs style to advanced pickers. His musical education came from years on the road playing a wide variety of musical styles—the kind of work that he says was his college education.

You might call Michael Schenkelberg, the current director of the Julie Davis School of Music at Swallow Hill, a different breed of cat. Michael is tall and strongly built, with a piercing gaze. He is soft-spoken but confident.

Born and raised in Cleveland Heights, Ohio, he first became interested in music during high school when an uncle gave him a twelve-string guitar. Shortly after that, Michael met Kevin Richards, considered something of a folk icon in northeast Ohio folk clubs. It was Richards who gave Michael his first fingerpicking lessons.

Michael attended a small, private high school and often went out to the local clubs, where he met the traditional bluesman Robert Lockwood Jr., who had learned blues from the famous Robert Johnson. Michael wanted to learn Lockwood's picking style and asked him to take him on as a student, but the irascible Lockwood turned him down and instead steered him back toward Kevin Richards.

After graduating from Iowa's Grinnell College with a major in biology and a minor in music, Michael spent time as a field biologist in Costa Rica studying endangered species, especially the beautiful scarlet macaw. He discovered that poaching was one of the primary causes endangering

Michael Schenkelberg joined Swallow Hill in 2007 and has brought a new level of energy to the Julie Davis School of Music. "There are no boundaries," he says. "It's all folk music." *Swallow Hill Music Association.*

the macaw, and he initiated community-organizing efforts to help save the birds. He eventually left Costa Rica when it became apparent that the guards at the park were behind most of the poaching.

Michael returned to Cleveland, where he found work as a substitute teacher in private schools, teaching a little bit of everything but mostly focusing on Latin, German and biology. He discovered he liked teaching and felt he was good at it; he was eventually offered a position at his old high school but turned it down for a job in Hawaii with Wilderness Adventures, where he taught backpacking and nature school. Through all of it, he played a little guitar, but in his own words, "Nothing seriously."

Upon returning to Cleveland a second time, he again taught school before becoming associated with his old guitar teacher Kevin Richards in a program called Blues in the Schools. The Rock and Roll Hall of Fame had been managing the program, but it had lost focus, so Richards and Schenkelberg took it over and worked relentlessly to bring it to the schools. Michael did a fair amount of research and grant writing while searching for program funding and thus gained an opportunity to study various education models that presented roots music. While carrying out the study, he came in contact with the Chicago Old Town School of Folk Music for the first time, and when a job as a camp counselor opened up there, he moved to Chicago to teach music and arts to five- to ten-year-olds. What he really had his eye on was a full-time teaching position, which finally opened up. He auditioned for a position teaching finger-style guitar, and as luck would have it, he knew many of the tunes by famous bluesmen like Mississippi John Hurt and Robert Johnson that were used in the class. He won the job.

Just as Michael was getting started at the Old Town School, he began working on another education project teaching folk music in schools throughout Ohio. Though he didn't really know the music at first, Michael dug in and learned the songs and put in serious time with his guitar. For a while, he traveled back and forth every week between Chicago and Ohio, working both jobs.

The Chicago Old Town School of Folk Music finally gave Michael a full-time teaching position. "I learned the Old Town teaching method more by osmosis," he said. "It came through discussions with other instructors rather than through formal presentation. And I learned the songs through the 'folk process'; that is, by listening."

In February 2007, he learned that the position of school director was open at Swallow Hill. He claims that he had but scant knowledge of Swallow Hill at the time, hearing vaguely that it was rather like the Old Town School of Folk Music, so on a whim, he threw together and submitted his résumé, thinking little about it. Swallow Hill called the next day, and he flew to Denver to interview with executive director Jim Williams, Julie Davis and Becky Miklitch. They immediately liked what they saw. The most interesting question they asked him was, "What is folk music?"

Michael's response to that elusive, pesky question sums up much about his worldview: "Folk music cannot be defined in specific musical terms. Folk music is more a *process* than music. Rap music is, in many ways, today's folk music. Folk music is not simply about preservation, though that is part of it. It's about bringing old and new musical forms together."

Michael landed the job and immediately used his strong sense of networking as he settled into his new home. Networking is where Michael's "community" begins; it's all about community in the end, and it is that spider webbing that is central to the folk process. "I think Swallow Hill has an image problem, and it revolves around the word 'folk,' which can sometimes be limiting. I want to make folk much broader in definition and more open. I want more diversity, especially when it comes to the younger crowd. We have to reach out and bring in young people."

Another of this "new breed" of Swallow Hill teachers is guitarist Aaron McCloskey. Born in Lexington, Massachusetts, in 1981, he took piano lessons for seven years, and unlike most kids, it was his idea, not his parents'. But it didn't really work; he never liked practicing. It was not until he entered Colby College, in Waterville, Maine, that music reentered his life. After his freshman year, Aaron decided to try guitar just for fun, and for him, it was. He studied hard and graduated with a degree in psychology and a passion for music.

His first stop after college was Meeker, Colorado, where he worked at the Elk Creek Lodge, one of Colorado's premier trout-fishing resorts. He spent a summer serving food and tending bar, which left plenty of free time to fish and play music. When the summer wound down, Aaron moved to Crested Butte to pursue his other interest: snowboarding. He worked in a local deli, boarded in the winter and fished in the summer. On the side, he taught a few guitar lessons, but it was hardly enough to keep food on the table. He ventured to west Texas to visit some friends who were studying at South Plains College in Levelland. South Plains, like most two-year schools, emphasizes career training for most of its students, but it also boasts one of the very few music programs where students can *study* bluegrass. Aaron found the program intriguing, and he was fascinated by two of its talented instructors, Alan Munde and Joe Carr. Oklahoma-born Munde played banjo with the bluegrass band Country Gazette for more than twenty years. Carr is an entirely self-taught guitarist who began playing at the age of thirteen, inspired by the legendary Doc Watson. In addition to guitar, Carr mastered the mandolin, fiddle, banjo and uke. He joined Country Gazette in the late 1970s and recorded a number of albums with the group. The band helped reshape the scope of bluegrass, making it "progressive" long before that term found common usage.

Captivated by the chance to work with and learn from Carr and Munde, Aaron enrolled in the two-year program. "I took a full class load of guitar, banjo and voice," he recalled. "I worked as a handyman, getting paid cash under the table, and it was enough to pay for tuition and rent, which fortunately was cheap. I had a nice-sized room but no TV. Still don't own one. If I wasn't in class, I was practicing. I spent ten to twelve hours a day playing."

After completing the program, Aaron packed up all his belongings in his car and headed back to Colorado. He wasn't sure what he would do, but he ended up in Lyons, where a number of his musician friends were living, and set about looking for work. "I called every school or music store in the phonebook, but there really wasn't much going on," he said. Then, by chance, he met Michael Schenkelberg and heard a little about Swallow Hill. He immediately set about investigating Swallow Hill and soon interviewed for a teaching position. "It was just good timing. I had only been here a couple of months when the job came open."

Like other young teachers, Aaron likes the idea of new classes and new approaches and wants to expand Swallow Hill's offerings. "We're encouraged to come up with new offerings," he said, "so I liked the idea of classes in jazz and electric guitar. I'm constantly encouraged to create new classes. The idea is to bring new people in and get other students returning." When asked if he considered himself a folk musician, Aaron answered, "I'm a musician, not a folk musician. I guess every kind of music is folk music. The idea here is to make a community of music by passing ideas along."

Swallow Hill has more than forty teachers, its unsung heroes who typically labor outside the public limelight but who touch students in a special way. They are a remarkable group of professionals.

GOING REALLY BIG:
WORLD'S BIGGEST GUITAR LESSON

When Tom Scharf challenged the staff to think bigger and "take it to the streets," Michael Schenkelberg took him at his word. And he had the experience. In 2007, while Michael was on the staff as a core guitar teacher, Chicago's Old Town School of Folk Music organized what it hoped would be the World's Biggest Guitar Lesson. It wanted to get into the *Guinness Book of World Records*. The record for simultaneous guitar playing was 1,683. A few months earlier, a horde of guitar pickers had banged out "Smoke on the Water" in Kansas City. The record for a music lesson stood at 539 people who participated in a mass harmonica tutorial in Switzerland. Old Town hoped to top them both.

It didn't quite meet its goal, but on August 7, 2007, an enthusiastic group of 1,377 guitarists of widely varying skills gathered at the Gazebo in Chicago's Wells Park, where they learned, fittingly, Hank Williams's "Jambalaya" and Woody Guthrie's "This Land Is Your Land." Record breaking or not, the lesson reached out to the community and drew plenty of media attention. Why not try it here?

Michael had the perfect venue in mind: Red Rocks Amphitheater. The Denver Film Society presented a summer series at the famous amphitheater called Film on the Rocks, hosted by Colorado Public Radio film critic Howie Movshovitz. Swallow Hill was responsible for booking acts that kicked the evening off with a forty-five-minute set of music before the evening feature film, which played on the four-story-high screen on the Red Rocks stage. Michael pitched the idea to the Denver Film Society. The society loved it.

Michael set about organizing the lesson and event. The Swallow Hill staff prepared and distributed flyers around town and circulated handbills to local schools, as well as various music schools. Both Swallow Hill and the Denver Film Society posted notices on their respective websites. Michael drew on his extensive experience teaching core guitar and created a twenty-minute lesson.

On Monday, August 18, 2008, an eager crowd began pouring into Red Rocks. Some twenty Swallow Hill volunteers—the organization's unsung heroes—directed the guitarists and musicians to the proper seating and, when needed, assisted them in tuning their instruments. Backstage, Michael coordinated a group of thirty local musicians who had volunteered to add their talents to the evening.

Denver-born bluesman Otis Taylor practically grew up in the Denver Folklore Center. He taught the nine hundred students at the World's (almost) Biggest Guitar Lesson at Red Rocks some basic blues riffs. *Swallow Hill Music Association.*

When the eight thousand attendees (not all musicians) were seated, Michael took the stage and began the lesson by making sure everyone was in tune. He started teaching the guitarists the 1973 Faces song "Ooh La La," selected because it is simple and accessible. It has a straightforward strum pattern and two chords that alternate each line. As he progressed through the lesson demonstrating the strums' rhythm pattern and chord changes, the lyrics and chords appeared on the gigantic screen behind him. Fortunately, most of the guitarists already had some knowledge of the instrument and had little trouble keeping up.

As the players became more comfortable with the song, other Denver-area musicians, including Otis Taylor and Rich Moore, joined him on stage, adding a variety of supporting parts. By the end of the lesson, there were nine hundred guitarists in the audience strumming away, joined by others who had brought ukuleles, French horns, a harmonium, at least one sitar and a full marching band. And eight hundred voices singing as loud as they could.

They did not break the world record, but they did make some beautiful noise. In Michael's words, the project served to "project a 'new image' for Swallow Hill, something beyond their restrictive folk music image. My idea is to build community and use music as the tool not the end." It isn't clear how many remember the evening's film (it was the Ben Stiller comedy *Zoolander*), but they won't likely forget the experience.

UKES GALORE

During the 1990s, the ukulele experienced a sudden resurgence in popularity, something few music pundits would have predicted. Hawaiian music was widely popular from 1915 to 1930, and America happily took to the uke; it was small, portable, inexpensive and, with only four strings, relatively easy to learn to play simple songs. Many vaudevillians included the uke in their acts, but by the 1950s, the instrument had lost much of its mainstream popularity. Arthur Godfrey strummed it on his television show, but with the rise of rock-and-roll, kids shunned the uke in favor of the guitar. Oddly, in the midst of the rock guitar explosion of the 1960s, George Harrison of the Beatles loved the uke. He owned dozens of them, often making them gifts to his best friends.

The ukulele revival started quietly in the 1990s and gained momentum as a coterie of young virtuosos demonstrated that the ukulele, in spite of its

Ukulele players at Swallow Hill's UkeFest, one of the most popular annual events on the calendar. *Swallow Hill Music Association.*

seemingly limited two-octave range, was more versatile than many believed. One of the new uke masters is Jake Shimabukuro (b. 1976), the Hawaiian-born virtuoso whose spectacular versions of jazz, funk, classical, rock, folk and bluegrass classics put images of Don Ho and swaying palm trees to rest. Hearing Shimabukuro play "While My Guitar Gently Weeps" or "Stars and Stripes Forever" will leave a new listener shaking his head.

Swallow Hill caught the uke wave early on and began offering an ever-expanding range of classes for kids and adults, from beginners to advanced students. In 2010, the Denver City Parks Department asked Swallow Hill to stage an event to help celebrate the reopening of the refurbished Ruby Hill Park in Southwest Denver. Michael Schenkelberg thought he had the perfect package: the World's Biggest Uke Lesson. The Parks Department liked the idea and agreed to erect a stage at Ruby Hill Park where Swallow Hill could present the lesson and hire the entertainers. They hoped to beat the record of 852, which was set in 2009 at the London Ukulele Festival. No experience necessary. The event would also help kick off the 2010 edition of Swallow Hill's own successful UkeFest.

To make the lesson more enticing, Michael came up with an interesting twist: why not make ukes available to those who wanted to learn to play but did not own an instrument? With that in mind, he wrote a grant request to the Scientific and Cultural Facilities Tax District requesting $10,000 to purchase ukes for this cultural outreach effort. SCFD agreed. With the grant in hand, Swallow Hill staffers had to hustle to find hundreds of ukes. No store had that many in stock, of course, and few distributors kept that many on hand, but they finally located a distributor able to fill an order for four hundred ukuleles.

On September 25, 2010, Denver mayor John Hickenlooper opened the festivities, which included a local chef competition. Uke and would-be uke players of all ages flocked to Ruby Hill Park. Denver's own uke virtuoso, Ukulele Loki, led the lesson. They didn't quite break the record, but 138 uke players brought their instruments, and another 274 people took advantage of the loaner ukes, making the lesson the third largest ever. Ukulele Loki taught the crowd Roger Miller's chestnut "King of the Road," and a free live concert with Patty Larkin and Lucy Kaplansky followed the lesson.

Michael grins when he talks about the uke, which is now the second most popular instrument at Swallow Hill's Julie Davis School of Music. "We love 'em!" he says. "I call the uke our 'gateway drug' since it'll get people hooked on making music. What could be better than that?"

Michael has his eye on another target: World Music Day, June 22. He envisions a music lesson simultaneously presented by music schools like Swallow Hill, Chicago's Old Town School of Folk Music, Passim and others, coordinated through satellite hook-ups. It's hard to imagine how many students might sign up for that, but it gives new meaning to the word "community."

9

Bringing It All Back Home

The Community

By the early 1990s, Harry Tuft was reconsidering his options. He had kept his passion for music alive by serving diligently on Swallow Hill's board since the mid-'80s. On the other hand, he had tried his hand at a variety of jobs, none of them fully satisfying. He finally considered the possibility of resurrecting the Folklore Center.

Much had changed in the decade or so since closing the DFC. The times had changed; Denver and its music scene had changed. Denver was bigger and even more cosmopolitan, and the music scene had flourished, with new venues featuring all kinds of newer music from dance to rap and hip-hop, but there was less emphasis on acoustic music. Most of all, Harry had changed. He had opened the original Denver Folklore Center in 1962 because he believed that Denver *needed* such a facility to serve a burgeoning acoustic music community. After the DFC closed, Swallow Hill filled some of the same services for the same community. "When I opened the second time," Harry recalled, "there was a need in *me* for a store of that kind. I realized that of all the things that I had done, it was the one that had given me the most pleasure, which was what I was the best at." He paused, looked down at his hands and then humbly added, "I wasn't very good at anything else."

Harry searched through many Denver neighborhoods seeking a suitable site, and as luck would have it, he was able to secure the building at 1893 South Pearl, just across Jewell Street to the north of Swallow Hill's facility. Working with some of his longtime friends, he outfitted the new store so that it had the same warm, welcoming feel of the original on Seventeenth Avenue, and he proudly reopened the Denver Folklore Center in March

1993. With Swallow Hill just fifty yards away, he re-created much of the same synergy of store, performance and school that he had originated on East Seventeenth.

Harry's original efforts at promoting music, acoustic instruments and accessories inspired other entrepreneurs to follow in his steps after the closure of the first DFC. Two of Denver's most successful music stores dedicated to acoustic instruments, the Olde Town Pickin' Parlor in Arvada and Acoustic Music Revival on South Broadway, mimicked the feel and atmosphere of the DFC, though neither had pursued concert promotion or provided nearly as much in the way of musical education. Today, the Denver Folklore Center continues at its Pearl Street location, even though Swallow Hill moved to its Yale Avenue building in 1999. Those who remember the original store often remark that the new store looks the same. It doesn't, but it does exude the same homey feel.

Harry's vision of combining a store, instrument repair shop, school, concert space and performance promotion was unique locally and nationally when he opened the original store in 1962. Other instrument merchandisers specializing in acoustic stringed instruments, including Mandolin Brothers in Staten Island, Gruhn Guitars in Nashville and Elderly Music in Lansing, Michigan, are all considerably larger and better known nationally but focus almost entirely on instrument sales. And all have developed substantial mail-order and Internet-based businesses, while the DFC remains largely locally focused. If anything threatens these local establishments, it is the growth of the even larger Internet-based stores and their gargantuan counterparts, the guitar superstores, that put an emphasis on price rather than personal service.

Longtime customers continue to look to the DFC as their source for instruments and recordings. New customers find solid, honest advice on instrument purchases and can quietly browse its extensive collection of folk-oriented sheet music and instruction manuals. When customers purchase an instrument from Harry, they feel as if they made a friend. More than anything, the Folklore Center remains the focal point for those interested in acoustic music, and that unique sense of community permeates the store. Locals drop in just to visit, and touring musicians stop by to catch up with old friends, to find a bit of escape from the rigors and insanity of the road or to get that emergency repair they need to a piece of essential gear. After fifty years, the DFC remains a Denver cultural and social landmark.

DEEP COMMUNITY

Most historians place the folk revival between 1940 and 1970. A few of those historians focus more on the arc of the commercial popularity of folk music, dating the revival between 1950 (starting with the Weavers) and ending in 1975. Regardless of the dates, much has happened in the ensuing four decades since the revival's end. New York may have been the genesis of much that happened during the folk revival, but with its emphasis on commerciality, many of its "folk places" have disappeared entirely or morphed into something different. The New York Folklore Center closed its doors in 1973. Disillusioned with America, its politics and the dying folk scene, Izzy Young moved to Sweden. Most of the Greenwich Village folk clubs are gone. Matt Umanov Guitars survives on Bleecker Street while all the other stores have faded away. The big music conglomerates have gobbled up all the record labels that once highlighted folk music. Only Moe Ashe's Folkways Records, now under the auspices of the Smithsonian Institute, remains committed to its founder's vision of cultural preservation.

Through it all, a small group of folk music–oriented organizations has managed to persist in the face of relentless change. The Chicago Old Town School of Folk Music—granddaddy of 'em all—founded in 1957, continues to thrive. It operates the largest school dedicated to folk music styles in the country, serving more than six thousand students annually, and another eighty-five thousand listeners attend

Born in Scotland, Bert Jansch was one of the major forces in British folk music. His fingerpicking style meshed perfectly with John Renbourn in their group Pentangle in the 1960s and '70s. He brought his jazz-inflected guitar to Swallow Hill often. *Swallow Hill Music Association.*

its concert series each year. In 2011, Old Town was in the midst of a substantial expansion project.

The Ark in Ann Arbor, Michigan, is another nonprofit survivor. Founded in 1965, it is now in its third location, where it places an emphasis on concert presentation while offering selected music classes and workshops to its faithful customers.

Club Passim in Boston's historic Harvard Square has deep roots and history. It originated in 1958 as a jazz spot called Club 47 but quickly thereafter became *the* New England folk club. Many wonderful talents got their professional starts at Club 47, including Joan Baez, Tom Rush and Eric "Rick" Von Schmidt. In the late 1960s, Club 47 morphed into Passim and continued as a small venue featuring all types of acoustic music. It incorporated as the nonprofit Club Passim in 1994 and carries on today, presenting over two hundred shows a year and featuring a small school of some five hundred students.

With Swallow Hill Music Association and the reconstituted Folklore Center, Denver proudly belongs to this small, hardy band of music pioneers who have survived fifty-plus years of tectonic shifts in music tastes.

The obvious question, of course, is why? In a world possessed by newer, bigger and better, where the latest techno gizmos with dwindling half-lives clamor for the public's ever-shrinking attention span, why have these organizations survived—even thrived—when most others have not? There is mostly just opinion on this issue, but many people think that folk music now has the same appeal of authenticity that it had sixty years ago. For many fans, it is just more real, less manufactured. In the fast-paced electronic world, some people find comfort in music whose roots go back hundreds of years and embrace all cultures. And many people want to *make* their own music, and these places offer schools and the opportunity to meet other like-minded musicians, as well as opportunities to perform.

"It may be a lot of things," says Tom Scharf, "but Swallow Hill has never been a building; it's the people. That's what matters."

He has a point. Most of the businesses—record companies, clubs, stores—that have disappeared were built around profit. Swallow Hill and its fellow folk music nonprofits worry just as much about revenue and expenses as they ever did, but they survive because their founders and members are passionate about music. And the community. "I think a lot of it is the idea of belonging to something that has a purpose and is bigger than you," Scharf reflected recently.

Roger McGuinn played back up for the Chad Mitchell Trio, Judy Collins and Hoyt Axton before founding the pioneering folk-rock group the Byrds, which influenced everyone. His shows feature his fine songs and classic jangly twelve-string guitar style. *Bill Kollar.*

The Swallow Hill community is diverse. It includes the students who take classes here but do not necessarily attend concerts. It also includes the concertgoers who are not musicians or at least don't attend classes. Then there are the teachers, of course, and the administrative staff and board members. And the general public who attend our bigger shows and the students in Denver-area schools where our Traveling Troupe performs. That's a "formal definition" of our community.

But there is a broader community that extends well beyond these boundaries. A story from 2010 about a number of people who did not even know one another might serve to illustrate the power and meaning of that community.

It involves multi-instrumentalist Kenny Edwards, who was born in 1946 and grew up in Santa Monica. In the late 1960s and early '70s, Southern California proved to be a hotbed of musical invention where the crosscurrents of folk, country, bluegrass and rock intermingled to produce, among others, the Eagles, Poco, Jackson Browne and Warren Zevon. Early on, Edwards teamed up with Tucson transplant Bob Kimmel and vocalist

Linda Ronstadt to form the group Stone Ponys, whose debut release is considered a masterpiece by many, even though it produced no hits. They recorded a second album, but the group disbanded just before they were about to tour, and their record company withheld the album's release.

The doe-eyed Linda Ronstadt, in the meantime, went on to score a couple of minor hits with "Different Drum" and "Long Long Time," while Edwards chose to work with singer/songwriters Wendy Waldman, Andrew Gold and Karla Bonoff. All were gifted writers and singers, and each harbored aspirations of individual careers yet enjoyed singing together. They eventually decided to form the group Bryndle, signed a record contract and recorded an album, but it never saw the light of day.

In 1974, Ronstadt, trusting her old band mate's musical taste and ability, approached Edwards and asked him to rejoin her band and, hopefully, reignite her career. It worked. The talented Edwards acted as her band leader and bass player, brought in Andrew Gold to play keyboard and produced a five-year string of hits that included "You're No Good," "When Will I Be Loved," "Heat Wave," "Blue Bayou" and "It's So Easy," which all cracked the Top Ten and made her an international star. They toured extensively during Ronstadt's glory years. In the role of producer, Kenny Edwards took control in the recording studio, where he delivered his considerable multi-instrumental talents in addition to adding vocals and sharing songwriting credits. He went on to produce albums by Wendy Waldman and Karla Bonoff and added film and TV production credits, including *Miami Vice* and *The Street*.

In spite of his central role in the development of country rock, Kenny Edwards never became a household name, except to people in the industry and inveterate readers of liner notes. From the 1980s on, he lent his instrumental and arranging skills to others, most frequently touring with Karla Bonoff. Most of all, he simply liked to play music. "He'd show up for an open mic night at Swallow Hill, and there'd be eight or ten people there to play, most of them lacking in real talent," Tom Scharf recalled. "I'd ask him why he was playing here, and he'd say that it was the idea of getting out and playing that was important, not the talent level. This was an important part of his 'community.'"

Kenny Edwards arrived in Denver as part of Karla Bonoff's band for an August 2010 concert date at Denver Botanic Gardens. He didn't look well and felt worse, complaining that he was constantly tired. Unknown to most people, including many of his friends, he had been receiving chemotherapy for prostate cancer. The day before the show, he went to emergency services, where the medical team performed a battery of tests that indicated he was suffering from the blood disorder TTP (thrombotic thrombocytopenic purpura). The prognosis was not good, and there was little the medical team could do for him. Upon hearing the news, Kenny said he just wanted to go home to Santa Monica and his family, but the doctors would not release him unless he made the trip by air ambulance, which would cost $25,000. He simply didn't have that kind of money. Swallow Hill, cosponsor of the show, felt that it had to try to do something for this outstanding musician, and it placed a fundraising appeal on its website. A number of people responded, but Swallow Hill remained far away from collecting the needed $25,000. Karla Bonoff performed her show without her good friend.

While Edwards lingered in the hospital wondering if he would ever see his home and family again, singer/songwriter Marc Cohn arrived in Denver for his Botanical Garden date. Cohn, a native of Cleveland, Ohio, and a graduate of Oberlin College, struck musical gold with his 1991 hit "Walking in Memphis" and had continued to play concerts to avid fans. His return to Denver was fraught with emotion, but not because of music or stage fright. On August 7, 2005, after a Denver concert with Suzanne Vega, Cohn was shot in the head during an attempted carjacking in Denver's LoDo district. Miraculously, the bullet did not pierce his skull, and he was able to leave the hospital the following day, quite seriously shaken.

On the day of his 2010 Botanic Gardens show, Cohn made a point to retrace his steps on that fateful night. He revisited Denver's Lower Downtown, where he very nearly met his end, claiming that he needed to connect to the place on a spiritual level, that he could not simply avoid it and block it out as if it had never happened. Before the show, he shared his story with Swallow Hill's executive director, Tom Scharf. Touched by the story's haunting power, Tom told Marc about Kenny Edwards and his dilemma. Marc did not know Kenny; they had never met. But he thought about it before going on that evening.

Cohn took the stage that night and played with a passion that comes rarely to an artist, and his audience loved it. About midway through the program, he slipped off his guitar and put it down, took the microphone from its stand and walked to the front of the stage. He then quietly told the rapt audience about Kenny's medical condition and his dilemma. Wasn't there something this beautiful crowd of people might do for a fine fellow musician in need? Personal appeals often fall on deaf ears. Most often individuals feel powerless to make much of a difference.

When the show was over and as the musicians and crew were packing up their gear, a man approached the stage. He said that he was the pilot of an air ambulance and that he and his crew had truly enjoyed the evening's performance. He went on to say that he and his crew were available the next day; they would be pleased to fly ailing Kenny Edwards home to California. Three days later, on August 18, Kenny Edwards passed away in his Santa Monica home.

The pilot and crew were not looking for special recognition. Indeed, they were simply part of Swallow Hill's extended community, and they were merely making a unique contribution. This community's bonds run deep in Denver.

IF I HAD A SONG

In 2011, *Sing Out! The Folk Music Magazine* celebrated a notable milestone. For sixty years, this exceptional publication has maintained its "mission to preserve and support the cultural diversity and heritage of all traditional and contemporary folk musics, and to encourage making folk music a part of everyday lives." It didn't start out that way.

After World War II, some artists and enthusiasts looked for a way to combine music with political activism. Pete Seeger, Woody Guthrie, Lee Hays and Irwin Silber, among others, formed People's Songs, Inc., with the idea to publish a monthly magazine to promote their ideas. In May 1950, the first issue of *Sing Out!* hit the streets, borrowing the name from Pete Seeger and Lee Hays's "The Hammer Song."

Sing Out! weathered—just barely—the dark McCarthy and HUAC years of the early 1950s and even survived the heady 1960s, when folk music rode its commercial high. It was among the first to recognize Bob Dylan's substantial talents, and circulation topped twenty-five thousand. It was a temporary high; debt and flagging circulation almost brought the magazine to its knees, but a hardy group of editors, writers and readers would not let the magazine die.

To celebrate its sixtieth anniversary, *Sing Out!* editor Mark D. Moss compiled a folk forum, asking sixty notable figures in the folk world to give their comments and random thoughts on folk music and its community. Remarkably, two dominant ideas emerged from the sixty diverse respondents: accessibility and community. Many wrote about their first encounter with the music, its energy and the idea that it looked accessible; that is, the music appeared simple enough for anyone to perform. It isn't, of course, but it encouraged many to try their hand at it, and many succeeded beautifully. Accessibility is what keeps the music alive as the generations change.

After fifty years serving Denver's music community, Harry Tuft summed it up rather nicely. Harry wrote, "Music is the mortar between the bricks of our society wall, and folk music is a strong ingredient in that mortar. It helps bring folks together. Community is strengthened by it, and we need community."

No one can predict where folk music and its community will be in another fifty years, of course, but if music holds any power at all, each new generation will hear the music that came before and build on it. It should be in good hands.

BIBLIOGRAPHY

PRIMARY SOURCES
Author Interviews

Chris Daniels, tape recording, Denver, CO, September 21, 2005.

Julie Davis, tape recording, Denver, CO, June 28, 2006.

Richard Lamm, e-mail, Denver, CO, February 8, 2005.

Rebecca Miklitch, tape recording, Denver, CO, May 24, 2006.

Tom Scharf, tape recording, Denver, CO, October 23, 2011.

Larry Shirkey, tape recording, Aurora, CO, March 20, 2005.

Harry Tuft, tape recording, Denver, CO, February 3; March 18; April 18, 2005.

Seth Weisberg, tape recording, Denver, CO, September 28, 2006.

Dick Weissman, tape recording, Denver, CO, September 21, 2005.

Jim Williams, tape recording, Denver, CO, May 8, 2006.

Newspapers and Periodicals

Hause, Butch. "Folk Music Friends Remember Ferretta." *Denver Post*, March 11, 1993.

Kreck, Dick. "Grubstake Relives Its Carefree Folk Music Days." *Denver Post*, May 29, 1994.

Moss, Mark D. "Sing Out! 60 for 60, Part IV." *Sing Out!* 54, no. 2 (Spring 2011).

Swallow Hill Music Association Newsletter. Spring 1987.

SECONDARY SOURCES

Unpublished Documents

Fish, Larry, and Larry Goldman. "A History of Swallow Hill Music Association." http://www.fountainware.com/misc/book.htm (accessed with permission from the authors, September 10, 2005).

Books

Cantwell, Robert. *When We Were Good: The Folk Revival*. Cambridge, MA: Harvard University Press, 1996.

Carter, Walter. *The Martin Book: A Complete History of Martin Guitars*. San Francisco, CA: GPI Books, 1995.

Cohen, Ronald D. *Rainbow Quest: The Folk Music Revival and American Society, 1940–1970*. Amherst: University of Massachusetts Press, 2002.

Collins, Judy. *Trust Your Heart: An Autobiography*. New York: Houghton Mifflin, 1987.

Cray, Ed. *Ramblin' Man: The Life and Times of Woody Guthrie*. New York: W.W. Norton and Company, 2004.

Denisoff, R. Serge. *Great Day Coming: Folk Music and the American Left*. Urbana: University of Illinois Press, 1971.

————. *Songs of Protest, War & Peace: A Bibliography and Discography*. Santa Barbara, CA: ABC-Clio, 1973.

Dylan, Bob. *Chronicles: Volume One*. New York: Simon and Schuster, 2004.

Filene, Benjamin. *Romancing the Folk: Public Memory & American Roots Music*. Chapel Hill: University of North Carolina Press, 2000.

Friedlander, Paul. *Rock and Roll: A Social History*. Boulder, CO: Westview Press, 1996.

Glazer, Tom. *Songs of Peace, Freedom, and Protest*. New York: D. McKay Co., 1970.

Greenway, John. *American Folksongs of Protest*. New York: Octagon Books, 1953. Reprint, 1971.

Guthrie, Woody. *Bound for Glory*. New York: Penguin Books, 1943.

————. *The Woody Guthrie Songbook*. New York: Grosset & Dunlap, 1976.

Hajdu, David. *Positively 4th Street: The Lives and Times of Joan Baez, Bob Dylan, Mimi Baez Fariña, and Richard Fariña*. New York: North Point Press, 2001.

Johnson, Richard, Dick Boak, and Mike Longworth. *Martin Guitars: A History*. Milwaukee, WI: Hal Leonard Corporation, 2008.

————. *Martin Guitars: A Technical Reference*. Milwaukee, WI: Hal Leonard Corporation, 2008.

Klein, Joe. *Woody Guthrie: A Life*. New York: Ballantine Books, 1980.

Lankford, Ronald D. *Folk Music USA: The Changing Voice of Protest*. New York: Schrimer Trade Books, 2005.

Lewis, George H., ed. *Side-Saddle on the Golden Calf: Social Structure and Popular Culture in America*. Pacific Palisades, CA: Goodyear Publishing Co., 1972.

Liberman, Robbie. *My Song Is My Weapon*. Urbana: University of Illinois Press, 1989.

Marcus, Greil. *Mystery Train*. New York: Dutton, 1990.

Marquesee, Mike. *The Wicked Messanger: Bob Dylan and the 1960s*. New York: Seven Stories Press, 2003. Reprint, 2005.

Moust, Hans. *The Guild Guitar Book: The Company and the Instruments, 1952–1977*. Milwaukee, WI: Hal Leonard, 1995.

Noel, Thomas J. *Sacred Stones: Colorado's Red Rocks Park & Amphitheatre*. Denver, CO: Denver's Division of Theatres & Arenas, 2004.

Rodnitzky, Jerome L. *Minstrels of the Dawn: The Folk-Protest Singer as a Cultural Hero*. Chicago: Nelson Hall, 1976.

Romanowski, Patricia, and Holly George-Warren, eds. *The New Rolling Stone Encyclopedia of Rock & Roll*. New York: Rolling Stone Press, 1983. Reprint, 1995.

Santelli, Robert, Holly George-Warren, and Jim Brown, eds. *American Roots Music*. New York: Harry N. Abrams, 2001.

Wald, Elijah. *Escaping the Delta: Robert Johnson and the Invention of the Blues*. New York: Amistad, 2004.

Weissman, Dick. *Which Side Are You On?: An Inside History of the Folk Music Revival in America*. New York: Continuum, 2005.

Whitburn, Joel. *The Billboard Book of Top 40 Hits*. New York: Billboard Publications, 1983.

Zwonitzer, Mark, and Charles Hirshberg. *Will You Miss Me When I'm Gone: The Carter Family and Their Legacy in American Music*. New York: Simon and Schuster, 2002.

Internet

About El Pomar. El Pomar Foundation, 2006. http://www.elpomar.org/page.asp?pageid=0|5&id=0|about_el_pomar.

About Swallow Hill. Swallow Hill Music Association, 2002. http://www.swallowhill.com/about/about_page.htm.

A Brief History. Old Town School of Folk Music, 2005. http://www.oldtownschool.org/history.

The Denver Folklore Center: Then and Now. Denver Folklore Center, 1999. http://www.denverfolklore.com.

Welcome to the City of Eugene Hult Center/Cultural Service. City of Eugene, Oregon. http://www.eugene-or.gov/portal/server.pt?space=Opener&control=OpenObject&cached=true&parentname=CommunityPage&parentid=0&in_hi_ClassID=514&in_hi_userid=2&in_hi_ObjectID=-214&in_hi_OpenerMode=2& (accessed October 28, 2006).

What Is SCFD. Scientific and Cultural Facilities District, 2006. http://www.scfd.org/about.shtml.

W.O.W. Hall: A Tribute to Eugene, Oregon's Music Legacy. W.O.W. Hall, 2006. http://www.associatedcontent.com/article/10481/wow_hall_a_tribute_to_eugene_oregons.html.

INDEX

A

Abbott, Steve 64
ABC television 58
Abilene Christian College 105
Acoustic Blues Festival 102
Acoustic Music Revival 134
Acuff, Roy 107
Adams State College 65
Adolph Coors 115
Alabama Sacred Harp Singers 71
Almanac Singers 24
Alvin, Dave 89
"Amazing Grace" 54
Amazing Rhythm Aces 85
Ambrosius, Bob 94, 96, 98
American Friends Service 41
American Records Distributors 33
Anderson, Bruce Leo 69, 70
Andrson, Bruce Leo 74
Anthology of American Folk Music 71
Ark, the 14, 136
Arnold, Joe 50
Arvada Center 64
ASCAP 101
Ashely, Clarence 71

Ashe, Moe 135
Ash Grove, the 27
Austin City Limits 57
Axton, Hoyt 137

B

Back Porch Majority, the 58
Baez, Joan 37, 39, 42, 43, 46, 48, 52, 58, 136
"Barbara Allen" 53
Barlow, Jerry 121
Barwick, Bill 30
Battlefield Band 84
Beat Generation 18
Beatles, the 46, 59
BeauSoleil 84
Bensusan, Pierre 104
Berklee College of Music 85
Berle, Milton 12
Berthoud Pass Lodge 19
Beverly Hillbillies, The 121
Birch, Doug 67
Bitter End, the 26
Blake, Nancy 62

Blake, Norman 30, 62, 107
"Blowin' in the Wind" 58
"Blue Bayou" 138
Bluebird Café 107
Blues in the Schools 124
BMH Synagogue 56
BMI 101
Bohren, Spencer 69
Bolin, Tommy 29
Bonnie and Clyde 121
Bonoff, Karla 138, 139
Bowers, Bryan 108
Brico, Dr. Antonia 52, 53
Brockett, Jaime 61
Broonzy, Big Bill 27
Brothers Four, the 26, 57, 58
Broussard, Sam 85
Browne, Jackson 107, 137
Brown, Roz 30, 60, 61, 66
Brown, Sam 56
Buckhorn Exchange 30
Burnell, Bruce 70
Burt, Gordon 104
Byrds, the 58, 137

C

Café, the 100
Café York 60
Cameron Church 76, 104, 118
Capitol Hill Community Center 65, 67
Carol, Bonnie 69
Carolina Tar Heels 71
Carr, Joe 125–126
Carson, Meredith 80, 84, 87, 88, 94,
     96, 102, 109
Carter Family, the 22, 58, 71
Chad Mitchell Trio, the 137
Chandler, Jon 122–123
Chatfield, Ray 39
Cherry Creek Gallery 62
Chicago Old Town School of Folk
     Music 14, 18, 19, 27, 36, 65,
     93, 94, 109, 124, 127, 131, 135
Church of the Nazarene 96

City Limits Bluegrass Band, the 46,
     121
"City of New Orleans, The" 30
City Park 62
Civilian Conservation Corps 45
civil rights 37, 39, 40, 58, 87
Clark, Guy 97
Close, Gordon 122
Club Passim 14, 136
clubs 18, 21, 26, 27–30, 52, 54, 81,
     105, 107, 123, 135, 136
CMT 75
Cockburn, Bruce 118
Cohen, Leonard 29, 54
Cohen, Ronald D. 18
Cohn, Marc 139
Colby College 125
Colgate University 77
Collins Calling 52
Collins, Charles 52
Collins, Judy 13, 19, 37, 46, 52–54, 58,
     59, 137
Colorado Academy 84
Colorado Governor's Award 95
Colorado Women's College 62, 63
Communist Party of the United States
     of America 17, 22–24
Community College of Denver 73
Conley's Nostalgia 29, 62
Conley, Walt 29
Contos, Pete 29
Cooney, Michael 63
Coors Foundation 95, 98
Corkin Theatre 62
Country Dinner Playhouse 114
Country Gazette 126
CPUSA. *See* Communist Party of the
     United States of America
Cranmer, George E. 43
Crary, Dan 84
Crosby, David 119
Crown Drug Store 33

D

Dan & Chaz 63
Daniels, Chris 84–104, 108
Daniels Hall 100, 104, 116
Dartmouth College 16
Davidson, Clinton 106
Davis, Julie 37–39, 40, 65–68, 70, 73, 95, 125
Decca Records 26
deFrancis, Kathy 61
deFrancis, Vince 40
Deliverance 121
Denisoff, R. Serge 22, 24
Denver Botanic Gardens 119, 138
Denver City Parks Department 130
Denver Film Society 127
Denver Folklore Center 8, 14, 15, 16, 31–52, 55–56, 60, 61, 65, 66, 85, 121, 122
  concerts at 42
  expansion 41
  interior 32
  music lessons 35–36
  Pearl Street 133–134
Denver Foundation 83
Denver, John 58, 77
Denver Magazine 62
Denver Mayor's Award 95
Denver Mountain Parks 43
Denver Musicians Union 56
Denver National Bank 50
Denver Police Department 52
Denver Post 121
Denver Savings Bank 31
Denver University 115
DFC. *See* Denver Folklore Center
"Different Drum" 138
Dillards, the 121
Dimichalis, Susan 95
Disney, Walt 11
Dobrolic Plectoral Society 107
Douglas, Jerry 84
Downing, George 33
"Dueling Banjos" 121

dulcimer 67, 69
Dylan, Bob 13, 40, 42, 47, 54, 58, 71, 140

E

Eagles, the 137
East High School 37, 52, 53, 54, 65
Ebbets Field 29, 60
Eberthardt, Cliff 90
Ed Sullivan Show, The 59
Edwards, Kenny 137–140
Elderly Music 48, 134
Elektra Records 33, 54
Elitch Gardens 91
Elk Creek Lodge 125
Ellie Caukins Theatre 118
Elliott, Ramblin' Jack 34, 46, 62
El Pomar Foundation 95
"End Is Not in Sight, The" 85
"Engine 143" 71
Eugene Performing Arts Center 108
Events Center 62
Executive Tower Inn 29
Exodus 19, 29, 54, 60

F

Faces, the 129
Farina, Richard 58
Faro, Rachel 62
Ferretta, David 41, 47, 61
Ferretta's Global Village 41, 62, 121
Ferris, Matt 39
First Denver Folk Festival 63
First Unitarian Church 62
Fish, Larry 94
Five Points 21
Flatt and Scruggs 58, 121
Flower, Mary 63, 70, 101
"Foggy Mountain Breakdown" 121
Folkathon 98, 100
Folkways Records 26, 33, 135
Forster, Nick 64
Fracasso, Michael 84

"Frankie" 71
Frisell, Bill 46

G

Gabriel, Peter 75
Garcia, Tony 76
Gaslight 26
Gate of Horn 54
Gates Foundation 95, 98
Gateway Singers, the 26
Gavan, Steve 94
Geer, Will 17
General Electric 94
Generic Bluegrass 61
Gerde's Folk City 26, 54
Geremia, Paul 103
Gibson, Bob 54
Gibson, Dave 93
Gibson Guitars 33, 35
Gilbert, Ronnie 17, 24
Gilded Cage, the 17
Gilmore, David 119
Gold, Andrew 138
Goodman, Steve 30, 57
"Good Night Irene" 26
Graceland 75
Grateful Dead, the 107
Great Depression 23
Greenhill, Manny 42, 46
Green Spider 29, 31, 41, 52, 60
Greenwich Village 18, 26, 54, 135
Gregson, Clive 84
Griffith, Nancy 118
Grinnell College 123
Grossman, Albert 42
Grubstake 63, 64, 84
Gruhn Guitars 134
Guard, Dave 26
Guild Guitars 35
Guinness Book of World Records, The 127
Gurtler, Sandy 91
Guthrie, Arlo 45, 46
Guthrie, Woody 17, 23, 24, 26, 54,
    127, 140

H

Happy Logan Music 35
Harlan County 23
Harrison, George 129
Hays, Lee 17, 24, 140
"Heat Wave" 138
Hee Haw 121
Hellerman, Fred 17, 24
Hendrix, Jimi 119
Heredia, Rene 63
Hewitt, Emmie 60
Hickenlooper, John 131
Hickler, Robert 94
"High Sheriff of Hazard, The" 58
Highwaymen, the 26, 57, 58
Hinojosa, Tish 84
Hip Help Center 50
Hirsch, Jim 93
Holtzman, Jac 54
Holy Cat 19
Hootenanny 54, 58
Hopkins, Lightning 106
Hot Rize 41, 46, 61, 62, 64, 101
"House Carpenter, The" 71
Houston, Cisco 17, 54
Hoyt, Burnham 43
HUAC 26, 140
Hungry i 19, 27
Hurt, Mississippi John 47, 71, 124

I

"I Ain't Marchin' Anymore" 58
Ian and Sylvia 12, 44, 57, 58
Ink Spots, the 12
Isenhart, Frank 93–94, 98
"It's So Easy" 138
Ives, Burl 17

J

"Jambalaya" 127
Jansch, Bert 135
Jennings, Waylon 57

Jewish Community Center 36
Johnson, Lyndon 57, 107
Johnson, Robert 123, 124
Jones, Ron 67
Journeymen, the 19
Joyner, Judith 74
Julie Davis School of Music 119, 122, 123, 131

K

Kaplansky, Lucy 131
KCFR 110
"Keep Your Eyes on the Prize" 39
Kelly, Alan 55, 60, 61
Kennedy, John F. 40
Kerr-Macey Studios 123
KFVD 23
KGNU 110
Kimmel, Bob 137
King, B.B. 87
"King of the Road" 131
Kingston Trio 13, 18, 19, 21, 26, 29, 57
Kirby, Rick 55, 56, 65
Knight-Campbell Music 35
KOMO 52
Krenz, Celeste 84
KVOD 66, 110
Kweskin, Jim 46

L

LaFave, Jimmy 84
Laird, Roy 67, 70
Lamar Tech 105
Lamm, Governor Richard 48–50, 59
La Petite Cafe 50
Larkin, Patty 131
Lead Belly 24, 26
"Leaving on a Jet Plane" 58
Ledbetter, Huddie. See Lead Belly
Led Zeppelin 119
Leo Instruments 69, 70, 75

Limelighters 26, 58
Lingo the Drifter 53
Linkletter, Jack 58
Lipscomb, Mance 106
Lockwood, Robert, Jr. 123
LoDo 92, 139
Lomax, Bess 17
Lombardo, Guy 12
London Ukulele Festival 130
"Long Long Time" 138
Louie, Louie 104

M

Magic Music 85
Mahal, Taj 42, 118
Maitch, Linda 69
Mamas and the Papas, the 19, 48–50
Mandolin Brothers 134
Marcus, Bob 46
Martinez, Ernie 120–123
Martin Guitars, C.F. 33, 35, 41, 55
Martin, James 94
MASH. See Swallow Hill Music Assocation
Matt Umanov Guitars 135
McAllister College 85
McCallum, Gerry 98
McCarthyism 17, 140
McCarthy, Senator Joseph 26
McCaslin, Mary 62
McCloskey, Aaron 125–126
McCreary, Bill 60
McCrimmon, Dan 61
McCutcheon, John 67
McDowell, Fred 47
McEuen, John 30
McGuinn, Roger 137
McMillan, Tom 60
MediaOne 115
Melody Music 122
Merchant Marines 17, 24
Meyer, Elissa 60
Miami Vice 138
"Michael Row the Boat Ashore" 58

Michael's Pub 54
Miklitch, Rebecca "Becky" 77–79, 80,
    81, 84, 87, 88, 92, 93, 94, 96,
    100, 102, 109, 122, 125
Miller, Austin 33
Miller, Roger 131
Mitchell, Joni 54, 107
Model Cities program 107
Moffatt, Katy 84
Monastery, the 62
Monroe, Bill 47
Mooney, Tom 23
Moore, Rich 61, 98, 129
Morris, Lynn 121, 122
Moss, Mark D. 140
Mother Folkers, the 63
Movshovitz, Howie 127
"Mr. Tambourine Man" 58
MTV 75
Muldaur, Geoff 46
Munde, Alan 125–126
Murphy, Michael Martin 30, 85
Music Man, The 120

N

Nash, Graham 119
National Aeronautics and Space
    Administration (NASA) 106
Nelson, Willie 57
Neustaedter, Hal 19, 27, 31, 52
New Christy Minstrels, the 58
New Left 17, 22
New Mexico Behavioral Health 114
New Mexico Jazz Workshop 108
Newport Folk Festival 42, 47–48
New York Folklore Center 18, 19, 27,
    33, 135
New York University 107
Niehouse, Eileen 67, 68, 73
Nitty Gritty Dirt Band, the 30
Nixon, Richard 57
NPR 110

O

Oberlin College 139
O'Brien, Molly 98, 99
O'Brien, Tim 64, 84, 99
Ochs, Phil 13, 47, 58
Okies 23
Olde Town Pickin' Parlor 123, 134
Old South Pearl Street BrewGrass
    Music Festival 119
Old South Pearl Street Brews and Blues
    Fest 119
Old Time Pickin' Parlor 107
Olympic Games 59
Oman, Joe 33
Oman, Lou 33
"Ooh La La" 129
Oregon County Fair 108
Outlaws, the 29
Oxford Hotel 29, 60

P

Paramount Theater 119
Paul Butterfield Blues Band 47, 48,
    108
Paxton, Tom 58, 84
Pearl Street Grill 93
Peer, Ralph 22
"Peg and Awl" 71
Penrose, Spence and Julie 95
People's Song Book, The 24
People's Songs, Inc. 140
Peter, Paul and Mary 21, 26, 40, 42,
    47, 57, 58
Phillips, Bruce "Utah" 63
Phillips, John 19, 48, 49, 50
Phipps Auditorium 46, 62
Pierson, Judith 108
Pink Floyd 119
Poco 137
Presley, Elvis 12
Price, Greg 61
Prine, John 57
punk 57

Purple Onion 27
Pyle, Chuck 104

R

Rambling Drifters 46, 61
Rau, Jerry 64
Red Channels 26
Redpath, Jean 84
Red Rocks Amphitheater 42–46, 127
Red Scare 26
Reece, Florence 23
Reed, Richard 67, 68
Regency Room 29, 30, 60
Renaissance Festival 108
Renbourn, John 84
Reynolds, Nick 26
Richards, Kevin 123, 124
Ringer, Jim 62
Riverside Records 26
Rock and Roll Hall of Fame 124
Rocky Mountain News 51, 61, 80
"Rocky Road" 71
Rodgers, Garnet 84
Rodgers, Jimmie 22
Ronstadt, Linda 138
Rooftop Singers 58
Root, Joseph Cullen 107
Roots & Branches 63
RootsFest 118, 119
Ruby Hill Park 130, 131
Rush, Tom 57, 108, 136
Ryman Auditorium 107

S

Samuelson, Maury 33
Sandberg, Larry 61
Satire Lounge 28, 29, 60
Sawtelle, Charlie 64, 101
SCFD. *See* Scientific and Cultural
        Facilities Tax District
Scharf, Matt 114, 115
Scharf's Services 113

Scharf, Tom 113–119, 127, 136–137,
        138, 139
Schenkelberg, Michael 110, 123–125,
        126, 127
Schumacher Accounting 93
Sciaky, Carla 67, 84
Scientific and Cultural Facilities Tax
        District 77, 87, 95, 109, 117,
        118, 119, 131
Second Denver Folk Festival 64
Seeger, Mike 34
Seeger, Pete 17, 24, 25, 26, 27, 39, 42,
        46, 58, 140
Shaffer, Deirdre 80
Shane, Bob 26
Shimabukuro, Jake 130
Shirkey, Larry 31–33, 37, 40, 42, 55,
        60
Shulgold, Marc 80
Silber, Irwin 140
Simon, Kit 123
Simon, Paul 75
Simple Gifts 64
Sing Out! 13, 42, 140
Skyloom Fibers 69
Smither, Chris 92
Smith, Harry 71
Smith, Russell 85
"Smoke on the Water" 127
Smothers Brothers 19, 27
So 75
"Someday Soon" 54
South Broadway Christian Church 91
South Plains College 125
Spark, The 104
Spoons 85
Stafford, Jo 53
Stajich, Steve 61
Stanesco, Jack 37, 40, 64
Stanley Brothers 47
Stanwood, Michael 61
Stapleton, Benjamin F. 43
"Stars and Stripes Forever" 130
State Electric Supply Company 71
Steve Allen Show, The 46

Stewart, John 29
Stinson Records 26
Stone Ponys 138
Street, The 138
Stribling, Mary 70
Sunday River Bluegrass Show 63
Su Teatro 76
Swallow, George R. 31
Swallow Hill Music Association 13, 14, 29, 55, 56, 57, 60–141
Swallow Hill Traveling Troupe 95, 102
Swallow Hill Troubadours 65
Sweet Georgia Brown 61
Sweet Loretta's 60, 121

T

Tabor Grand Opera House 21
Tarriers, the 26
Tattered Cover Book Store 70
Taylor, Otis 128, 129
Third Eye Theater 52
"Third Rate Romance" 85
"This Land Is Your Land" 127
Thorwardson, Nancy 64
"Tom Dooley" 12, 18, 26, 31, 57
Troubadour, the 27
Tuft Hall 100
Tuft, Harry 8, 14, 15, 16, 19, 26, 31–56, 59, 60, 61, 62, 63, 64, 66, 73, 78, 84, 85, 91–92, 92, 100, 116, 122, 133–134, 141
Tyler, Bob 98
Tyson, Ian 54
"Tzena Tzena" 26

U

UkeFest 130
ukulele 129
Ukulele Loki 131
University of Colorado 85
University of Denver 33
University of Hawaii 77

University of Houston 105
University of Massachusetts 114
University of Virginia 65
USWest 115

V

Vanguard Records 26
Vega, Suzanne 139
Vietnam War 39, 57, 106
Village Gate, the 26
Von Schmidt, Eric "Rick" 136

W

Wagner, Phyllis 39, 40, 46, 66
Waits, Tom 29
Waldman, Wendy 138
"Walking in Memphis" 139
"Walk Right In" 58
War on Poverty program 107
Washington University 71
Watson, Doc 29, 126
Weavers, the 17, 26, 52, 135
Weisberg, Seth 71–81, 83–84, 85, 87, 90, 94, 103
Weissman, Dick 17, 18, 19, 47
Welch, Kevin 84
Wells Music 35
Werblin, Stan 48
Wernick, Pete 64
"We Shall Not Be Moved" 39
"We Shall Overcome" 39
West Auditorium 62
Westbrooks, Wesley 47
Westword 83
"When Will I Be Loved" 138
"While My Guitar Gently Weeps" 130
White, Josh 24, 27, 40
Wilderness Adventures 124
Wildflowers 54
Wild Oats Market 93
Williams, Jim 105–112, 113, 118, 125
Williamson, Robin 84

Willie and Carol 69
Withers, Jeff 55, 60, 66
Wolf, John 66
Wolf, Kate 62
Wong, Janet 69
Woodmen of the World (WOW) 107
Woodstock Festival 46, 108
Works Progress Administration 45
World Music Day 131

Y

Young, Izzy 18, 19, 27, 135
"You're No Good" 138

Z

Zambrano, Joe 121
Zevon, Warren 137
Zither Shop 69
zydeco 75, 105

ABOUT THE AUTHOR

Paul Malkoski was born in Pennsylvania and grew up in West Virginia and Kentucky. He got his first guitar while in high school and learned to play from a Mel Bay teach-yourself-guitar book. Paul lived in New York City in the 1960s and in 1973 moved to Colorado, where he spent thirty years in the telecommunications business. He received his BA and MA degrees from the University of Colorado at Denver and currently teaches world and American history at Regis University and the Community College of Aurora. Paul worked at the Colorado Historical Society as a special project editor. He lives in Aurora, Colorado, with his wife, Mim, a middle school teacher, and their two French bulldogs. He is an avid guitarist, listens to music and attends concerts regularly. He enjoys reading, mostly history, and has a keen interest in Formula 1 motor racing. Paul has been a member of the Hole in the Wall Gang for twenty years.

Visit us at
www.historypress.net